SKILL-STREAM-ING IN EARLY CHILD-HOOD

TEACHING PROSOCIAL SKILLS TO THE PRESCHOOL AND KINDERGARTEN CHILD

Ellen McGinnis • Arnold P. Goldstein

RESEARCH PRESS COMPANY
2612 North Mattis Avenue
Champaign, Illinois 61821

Advisory Editor, Frederick H. Kanfer

Cover design by Jack Davis
Illustrations by Kathleen Jennings
Composition by Pam Frye Typesetting
Printed by McNaughton & Gunn

ISBN 0–87822–320–7
Library of Congress Catalog No. 90–60925

To Alex and Lauren, two very special preschoolers

Contents

Figures and Tables

FIGURES

TABLES

Acknowledgments

Thank you to the many teachers of preschool, kindergarten, and handicapped children who freely shared their concerns and experience – this book is clearly the better for their knowledge. Thanks also to our publisher, Ann Wendel, who through gentle prodding and encouragement provided the reinforcement needed to complete this manuscript. Karen Steiner, our editor at Research Press, has been a wise and patient counsel to this writing effort. She has our warmest appreciation. To friends and colleagues at North High School in Des Moines – Granville Williams, Sandy Frakes, Dick Moberly, and especially Leigh Lussie – thank you for truly making the journey easier. Ellen McGinnis's sister, Kathleen Jennings, gave not only her talent in providing the illustrations but also her support in this and other ventures. Finally, a loving thank you to Sara and Alex McGinnis for the many invaluable lessons they have provided. Their teachings, too, are reflected in this book.

CHAPTER 1

Introduction

The preschool and kindergarten years are a special time of wonder and change for the young child. But at the same time that social, language, and cognitive learning are rapidly taking place, most children also begin to experience anger, frustration, and fear – and to be confronted by increasing environmental demands. Consider the following scenarios:

- Leslie and Rob, age 4, are arguing about who will get the next turn on the preschool's new tricycle. Each one has hold of a handlebar, and neither seems likely to budge.

- Shauna, age 3, bursts into tears every time her mother encourages her to dress herself. "I can't do it!" she wails. And then, as she becomes even more frustrated and refuses to try, "I *won't* do it!"

- Will, age 6, never seems to have anyone to play with at recess. He shyly hangs around the other groups of kindergarten children but just doesn't appear to know how to become part of their games.

- Terry, age 5, often bullies her classmates to do what she says. "If you don't give me your scissors, I'll punch you," she orders. She usually gets what she wants, but the other children are afraid of her and avoid her whenever they can.

What these children lack, or are weak in, are the skills, abilities, or behaviors needed to be socially competent. In other words, such children are deficient in prosocial skills just as low achievers are deficient in academic skills. Many educational interventions have concentrated on decreasing inappropriate or undesirable social behaviors. However, it is not enough merely to teach young children what not to do; additional measures must be taken to teach them what they should do instead. The goal of this book is to provide teachers and others working with preschool and kindergarten children with a well-validated technique to systematically teach the behaviors necessary for effective and satisfying social interactions—in school, on the playground, and at home.[1]

This method, Skillstreaming, has already achieved success with both elementary-age children (McGinnis, Goldstein, Sprafkin, & Gershaw, 1984) and adolescents (Goldstein, 1973, 1981; Goldstein, Sprafkin, & Gershaw, 1976; Goldstein, Sprafkin, Gershaw, & Klein, 1980). Our extension of this method to children ages 3 to 6 is the result of growing awareness that, even at this early age, the mastery of prosocial skills plays a critical role in children's well being and later development.

The Preschool and Kindergarten Child

By 3 years, the age typically denoting the end of toddlerhood and the beginning of the preschool years, most young children are beginning to view themselves as part of a larger world—a world including demands that implicit and explicit skill competencies be mastered if the important adults in that world are to be pleased. Piaget (1962) has termed the ages between 2 and 7 the *preoperational stage*, a time when children begin to contemplate their actions and become increasingly aware of how their behavior brings about either desired rewards such as smiles, hugs, and words of praise, or undesired punishments such as frowns, reprimands, or loss of privileges.

Even though preschool and kindergarten children have acquired the desire both to please others and to avoid censure by acting in certain ways, many continue to think about how their behavior affects others only after they have reacted in an undesirable way. Although children at this age will likely be able to state the negative consequences of an already enacted behavior (e.g., "I made you sad"), they don't often think of the probable outcomes of the behavior before taking such action.

During these years, the young child is also making the transition from parallel play, in which he engages in independent play while a peer does likewise, to more interactive and cooperative play. Thus, social interactions become more frequent and complex (Hartup, 1983), and friendships become increasingly more important. Along with this increased

---

[1] Although the program described in this book is primarily geared toward children kindergarten age and younger, depending on the developmental level of the children involved, the skills and methods may be useful up through second grade.

frequency of social interaction comes the need for the young child to acquire a new set of skills. For instance, such skills include being able to deal successfully with conflict or arrange play with an unacquainted peer. Both of these skills have been found to predict children's friendship-making ability (Gottman, 1983).

Why Teach Prosocial Skills?

Why ought we be concerned with deficits in interpersonal or cognitive skills at this early stage of development? Such skill deficits have been the target of considerable research scrutiny. Studies suggest that problems in this area are related to school maladjustment (Gronlund & Anderson, 1959), peer rejection (Quay, 1979), and later delinquency (Roff, Sells, & Golden, 1972). Children with poor interpersonal skills, as compared to their socially competent peers, have been found to be at high risk for adjustment problems during both childhood (Green, Forehand, Beck, & Vosk, 1980; McConnell et al., 1984; Patterson, 1982) and adulthood (Cowen, Pederson, Babigian, Izzo, & Trost, 1973). In addition, the social competence of preschool children has been found to be predictive of their academic achievement in elementary school (Kohn, 1977).

Another central reason for teaching prosocial skills to young children concerns the new demands placed on them by the preschool or kindergarten setting. With this important change, children must all at once learn to get along not only with one or two siblings or neighborhood friends, but with an entire classroom of other children and adults. Also at this time, quite abruptly, adult and group demands become far greater. Children are now required to direct their attention to a selective activity, to sit among a group of other children in close proximity, to change activities according to an adult time frame, to follow a variety of instructions, and to interact cooperatively with other youngsters across a changing variety of tasks and settings. Such demands are not typically included in the home environment on a consistent basis. Therefore, the young child's first encounter with preschool or kindergarten typically involves a wide array of generally foreign skills and behaviors.

In this regard, Chan and Rueda (1979) describe a "hidden curriculum" operating within schools. This curriculum involves the assumption that all children enter the school setting with similar experiences and values. In other words, it is expected that children will have developed certain cognitive skills by exploring their environments and that they have acquired a set of student behaviors enabling them to respond appropriately to adult instructions. These assumptions appear to be faulty. Instead, teachers of preschool and kindergarten children encounter a very diverse group of individuals having different personalities and temperamental characteristics (Keogh & Burnstein, 1988), some who have had prior day care or preschool experiences and some who are entering a structured school setting for the first time. The cognitive and behavioral skills of children with less school experience may not be sufficient to meet the needs of the new, in-school situation.

Finally, it appears clear that even very young children can benefit from instruction in prosocial skills. In their work with preschoolers and kindergarten children, Spivack and Shure (1974) found that 4- and 5-year-olds can be successfully taught to identify alternative problem solutions, anticipate consequences, and use other problem-solving skills that have been found to enhance interpersonal adjustment. According to Maccoby (1980) these early years are the most critical ones for developing such prosocial behaviors as the ability to inhibit inappropriate behavior and to organize actions to achieve an external goal.

Who Benefits from Learning Prosocial Skills?

Three main groups of young children can benefit from systematic instruction in social skills: (1) children who are either withdrawn or aggressive; (2) children who are developing normally but who have periodic deficits in prosocial skill behaviors; and (3) children who have learning disabilities, communication disorders, behavioral problems, or other handicaps.

Withdrawal and aggression are the most salient reflections of prosocial skill deficit (Dowrick, 1986) and the ones most problematic for teachers and parents. Previously, it was thought that social isolation resulting from withdrawal naturally decreased as young children matured; therefore, children exhibiting such behavior did not generally receive active intervention. However, some researchers have found that social isolation may actually increase, rather than decrease, as children grow older (Hops, 1982; Oden, 1980). Little doubt exists that children who aggressively act out against the environment are at high risk for future problems (Coie, 1985; Parker & Asher, 1985) and that they will benefit from being taught constructive behavioral alternatives.

But what of the child who exhibits somewhat milder forms of these symptoms—the child who is otherwise developing normally but who may have periodic deficits in prosocial skill behaviors (Wanlas & Prinz, 1982)? Such periodic deficits may also interfere with the development of personal happiness and satisfying relationships with others. In addition, if reinforced consistently by significant persons in the youngster's life, problem behaviors have the potential to become more frequent and to generate even more negative outcomes. A related difficulty can result if the adults in the young child's world attempt to handle these negative outcomes for the child instead of teaching her how to deal with them herself. The social disadvantage of employing such a strategy is that the adult does the thinking for the child, thus taking away the opportunity for the child to solve her own problems and feel good about herself for her accomplishments (Spivack & Shure, 1974).

Finally, children who exhibit maladaptive and/or learning problems severe enough to cause them to be identified as handicapped are particularly good candidates for prosocial skills training. Deficits in the area of social skills have been observed in children with all categories of handicaps (Strain & Odom, 1986). In particular, several studies have clearly indicated that children with handicaps tend to interact with their peers less frequently and in more reciprocally negative ways than do children without handicaps (Allen, Benning, & Drummond, 1972; Bryan & Bryan, 1978; Strain, Shores, & Timm, 1977). Burstein (1986) found that preschoolers with handicaps interact more with teachers and less with other children than do their nonhandicapped peers. In addition, without active intervention, social skills deficits in early childhood tend to become even more disabling for many handicapped learners (Strain, 1981).

Mainstreaming for children with handicaps was mandated with the passage of Public Law 94–142, the Education for All Handicapped Children Act of 1975 (Federal Register, 1975). However, such attempts to educate children with handicaps "to the maximum extent appropriate" in the same classrooms as their nonhandicapped peers have often failed. These failures have largely been due to deficits in social behavior and educators' inability to attend adequately to their remediation (Gresham, 1981, 1984). Specific attention to the social needs of children ages 3 to 5 who have handicaps has been encouraged under an amendment to Public Law 99–457 (U. S. House of Representatives, 1986). This amendment provides funds for programs including activities and services to facilitate intellectual, emotional, physical, mental, social, language, and self-help skills.

What the Skillstreaming Program Involves

This book provides classroom teachers and others working with young children with a guiding strategy and concrete techniques for individual and group instruction in prosocial skills. Other potential users of the Skillstreaming method include resource teachers and school support personnel such as social workers, psychologists, and school counselors. Although the primary focus is on teaching in public school settings, counselors and teachers in mental health and residential facilities will also find this method appropriate and useful.

This book includes all the information necessary for planning and implementing prosocial skills instruction for preschool and kindergarten children. Chapter 2 gives the reader a detailed description of the components of Skillstreaming. Assessment procedures to assist educators in identifying children who are deficient in prosocial skills and in pinpointing skill strengths and weaknesses are presented in chapter 3. Chapter 4 details specific methods for planning and organizing Skillstreaming groups, and a detailed plan for implementation is described in chapter 5. Chapter 6 provides skill lesson plans for the 40 specific prosocial skills comprising the Skillstreaming curriculum, including the behavioral steps for each skill, suggested role-playing situations, and other information helpful in teaching and applying the skills. Specific techniques for managing individual and group behavior problems, along with a vignette illustrating the use of some of these techniques, are given in chapter 7. Finally, a separate Program Forms booklet provides skill checklists, record-keeping forms, skill step handouts, award forms, and other materials that can be freely reproduced and used in the group setting.

SUMMARY

In brief, we believe that teaching prosocial behavioral alternatives at an early age may enhance a child's personal development and may help prevent more serious difficulties in later childhood, adolescence, and early adulthood. Teaching prosocial skills is a valuable intervention for any child, with or without handicaps, mainstreamed or not, who shows the kind of undesirable behaviors or skill deficits that result in personal unhappiness, interpersonal difficulty, or academic ineffectiveness.

We believe teachers must not only make young children aware of social behaviors that are unacceptable, but must actually teach specific constructive alternatives as well. Preschoolers can be assisted in mastering daily school routines and can learn to follow through with adult expectations, to solve interpersonal conflicts, and to deal effectively with emotions. Just as we know we must teach youngsters to tie their shoes and understand that sounds are associated with the letters of the alphabet, so must we teach the behavioral skills that may lead to happier school, home, and neighborhood experiences.

CHAPTER 2

Components of Skillstreaming

Skillstreaming is a psychoeducational, behavioral approach for providing instruction in prosocial skills. It consists of (1) modeling, (2) role playing, (3) performance feedback, and (4) transfer training. Each skill to be taught is first broken down into its constituent parts or behavioral steps. Children are then shown examples of people (models) performing these behavioral steps competently. Next, the children rehearse or practice the skill steps they have observed (role playing), and receive feedback (e.g., approval or praise) from other children and the teacher as the role-played behavior becomes more and more like that of the model (performance feedback). Finally, a number of procedures are used that enhance the likelihood that the children will use these newly learned skills in real-life situations (transfer training). Each of these components will be discussed in detail in this chapter.

MODELING

Modeling, defined as learning by imitation, has been shown to be an effective teaching method for children and adolescents (Bandura, Ross, & Ross, 1961; Rogers-Warren & Baer, 1976; Rosenthal, 1976; Schneider & Byrne, 1985). Three types of learning by modeling have been identified.

One type is *observational learning,* or the learning of new behaviors not previously in the child's behavioral repertoire. Children often observe and imitate other children in the way they dress, talk, and behave. The use of new slang expressions, which filter through schools and neighborhoods, is one example of such learning.

Another type of learning involves *inhibitory* and *disinhibitory effects,* or the strengthening or weakening of behavior performed only rarely by the child. The behavior may be strengthened or weakened according to whether others are observed to be rewarded or punished for it. Children may see another child go unpunished or even rewarded for behaving rudely or aggressively and then react in a similar manner (disinhibitory effect). Alternatively, children may inhibit these reactions when they observe rude or aggressive behavior being punished (inhibitory effect).

Behavioral facilitation, or the performance of previously learned behaviors that are already within the child's behavioral repertoire and are positively received by others, is the third type of learning by modeling. For example, when a child has a toy or snack he seems to enjoy, a friend may then want one, too.

Research has demonstrated that many behaviors can be learned, strengthened, weakened, or facilitated through modeling. These behaviors include helping others, sharing, behaving independently, acting aggressively, acting nonaggressively, exhibiting certain speech patterns, interacting socially, and many more. It is clear that modeling can be an effective way of teaching people new behaviors. Yet it is also true that individuals observe a variety of behaviors that they do not then engage in themselves. For example, television, radio, magazines, and newspapers present very polished modeling displays of people buying products, but not everyone then buys those products. Children may see dozens, even hundreds, of behaviors enacted by peers in a typical day at preschool or kindergarten but copy only a few, or none, in response. Apparently, then, people learn by modeling under some circumstances but not others.

Research on modeling has identified several conditions that increase the effectiveness of the model, the modeling display, or the person observing the modeling. As discussed in chapter 5, much of the modeling in Skillstreaming is done live by the teacher. For this reason, it is critical that the teacher have a keen understanding of modeling and other qualities that enhance the potency of the modeling process.

Modeling Enhancers

Model characteristics

More effective modeling will occur when the model (1) seems to be highly skilled in the behavior, but not too highly skilled (i.e., a coping model is preferable over a mastery model); (2) is considered by the observer to be of high status; (3) is friendly and helpful; (4) is of the same age, sex, and social status as the observer; (5) controls rewards desired by the observer; and, of particular importance, (6) is rewarded for the behavior. In other words, we are all more likely to imitate powerful yet pleasant people who receive rewards for what they are doing, especially when the reward is something that we, too, desire.

Modeling display characteristics

More effective modeling will occur when the modeling display demonstrates the behaviors (1) in a clear and detailed manner; (2) in order from the least difficult to the most difficult; (3) with enough repetition to facilitate overlearning; (4) with little irrelevant detail; and (5) with several individuals serving as models.

Observer characteristics

More effective modeling will occur when the person observing the model, in this case the child, is (1) instructed to imitate the model; (2) friendly toward or likes the model; (3) similar in background to the model; and, especially important, (4) rewarded for performing the behaviors that have been modeled.

Research on Modeling

Research on modeling has shown it to be a particularly effective technique with children and adolescents. Specifically with respect to preschool children, modeling has been found to increase the social behaviors of smiling (Keller & Carlson, 1974), sharing (Alvord, 1978), frequency of social interaction (O'Connor, 1969), and displays of affection (Keller & Carlson, 1974). Bandura and his colleagues have demonstrated that young children do in fact exhibit more aggressive behaviors when vivid modeling displays of such behaviors are presented to them (Bandura et al., 1961). Such observational learning of aggression by children is a frequently replicated research finding (Fairchild & Erwin, 1977; Kirkland & Thelen, 1977; Rosenthal, 1976). In addition to enhancing the observational learning of aggressive behavior, modeling has been used successfully with children to teach such prosocial behaviors as social affiliativeness (Evers & Schwarz, 1973), creativity (Zimmerman & Dialissi, 1973), positive social interaction (Schneider & Byrne, 1985), self-control (Toner, Moore, & Ashley, 1978), sharing (Grusec, Kuczynski, Rushton, & Simutis, 1978; Rogers-Warren & Baer, 1976), certain cognitive skills (Lowe & Cuvo, 1976), and even imitation itself (Kaufman, Gordon, & Baker, 1978).

The positive outcome of modeling research indicates that modeling is a powerful teaching technique. If modeling is so effective, why then are the other Skillstreaming components (role playing, performance feedback, and transfer training) needed? The answer is clear: Modeling alone is not enough because its many positive effects are often very short lived. Learning appears to be improved when the learner has the opportunity and is encouraged to practice, rehearse, or role play the behaviors performed by the model and when the learner is rewarded for doing so. In other words, viewing the modeling display teaches the child *what* to do. In addition, she needs enough practice to learn *how* to do it and sufficient reward to motivate her or to let her know *why* she should behave in certain ways. The *how* question concerns the second component of Skillstreaming, role playing.

ROLE PLAYING

Role playing has been defined as "a situation in which an individual is asked to take a role (behave in certain ways) not normally his own, or if his own, in a place not normal for the enactment of the role" (Mann, 1956, p. 227). The use of role playing to help a person change his behavior or attitudes has been a popular approach in education for many years. For example, teachers of young children frequently direct their students in role playing stories and plays to assist in developing comprehension of content.

Role-Play Enhancers

As is the case for modeling, research impressively demonstrates the value of role playing for behavior and attitude change. However, as is also true for modeling, behavior or attitude change through role playing will be more likely to occur if certain conditions are met. These role-play enhancers include (1) choice on the part of the child regarding whether to take part in the role playing; (2) the child's commitment to the behavior or attitude she is role playing, which is fostered by the public (rather than private) nature of the role play; (3) improvisation in enacting the role-play behaviors; and (4) reward, approval, or reinforcement for enacting the role-play behaviors.

Research on Role Playing

Children participating in role playing at the preschool level have shown significantly more behavior and attitude change on such dimensions as sharing (Barton, 1981) and conflict management skills (Spivack & Shure, 1974) than have children merely observing a modeling display. In addition, role playing has been effective for other groups in increasing school attendance (Shoabs, 1964), social skills (Hubbel, 1954), acceptance of minority children (Nichols, 1954), interpersonal sensitivity in classroom settings (Chesler & Fox, 1966), attitudes toward another person (Davis & Jones, 1960), empathy (Staub, 1971), and a variety of other prosocial skills (Rathjen, Hiniker, & Rathjen, 1976; Ross, Ross, & Evans, 1976). Thus, it is clear that role playing can lead to many types of behavior and attitude change.

As with modeling, role playing may be seen as a necessary but insufficient behavior change technique. Its effects, as when modeling is used alone, often do not last (Lichtenstein, Keutzer, & Himes, 1969). Thus, in most attempts to help a child change his behavior, neither modeling nor role playing alone is enough. Combining the two is an improvement, but even this combination is insufficient, for the child still needs to know why he should behave in new ways. In other words, a motivational or incentive component must be added. Performance feedback, to be considered next, is therefore the third component of Skillstreaming.

PERFORMANCE FEEDBACK

Performance feedback involves providing the child with information on how well she has done during the role playing, particularly how well her enactment of the skill's behavioral steps corresponds to the model's portrayal of them. Feedback may take such forms as constructive suggestions for improvement, prompting, coaching, material reward, and, especially, such social reinforcement as praise and approval. For the preschool and kindergarten child, positive versus negative feedback will likely be most effective. Indeed, research with preschoolers has shown positive reinforcement to decrease aggression (Brown & Elliott, 1965; Slaby & Crowley, 1977; Wahler, 1967) and social isolation (Norquist & Bradley, 1973) and to increase cooperative skills (Norquist & Bradley, 1973; Slaby & Crowley, 1977).

Reinforcement typically has been defined as any event that serves to increase the likelihood that a given behavior will occur. Three types of reinforcement have been described: (1) material reinforcement, such as food or money; (2) social reinforcement, such as praise or approval from others; and (3) self-reinforcement, or positive evaluation of one's own behavior. (Table 1 lists a number of the material and social reinforcers available.) Effective performance feedback must give attention to all three types of reinforcement. Material reinforcement may be viewed as a necessary base, without which the higher levels of reinforcement (social and self-reinforcement) may not function. Indeed, material reinforcement may be the only class of reinforcement to which many young children will initially respond. However, because there is considerable evidence that behavior changed in response to a program of strictly material rewards typically disappears (extinguishes) when the material rewards are no longer forthcoming, and because social rewards are more likely to be available to the child outside of the training setting, the teacher should make an effort to pair material reinforcers with social reinforcers when providing positive performance feedback. The goal is subsequently to eliminate the material reinforcers while retaining the social rewards. In other words, it is important that a teaching effort not rely too heavily or too long on material reinforcers, although they may be necessary in the beginning stages of work with the young child.

TABLE 1 Material and Social Reinforcers

MATERIAL REINFORCERS		SOCIAL REINFORCERS	
Objects	**Activities**	**Nonverbal**	**Verbal**
Food (e.g., peanuts, raisins, apples, cereal) Stickers Stars Happy faces Awards Good notes home Ribbons Good work buttons Rubber stamp on hand Small toy or trinket Gum Photo of child	Feeding pets Watering plants Being first in line One-on-one time with teachers Extra free play Sharpening pencils Playing with a special toy Listening to a record Sitting at teacher's desk or chair Watching a special movie Extra outside play Using teacher's equipment (e.g., stapler, hole punch) Using colored chalk on blackboard Choosing a story to be read to the class Turning lights on or off Earning a puzzle piece (completing the puzzle when all are earned) Listening to a story on a tape recorder Using a typewriter or computer Using the telephone	Smiling Hugging Looking interested Physical closeness A pat on the back A wink Nodding Arm around the child Holding hands	Good listening, good thinking, etc. Thank you. Wow! I really like that. That was nice. You really waited. Nice job. Terrific. Great,____!

Even though in real life social reinforcers may be more available than material reinforcers, it is also true that many valuable real-life behaviors go unnoticed and unappreciated. Therefore, social reinforcement alone may at times be an unreliable ally in the teaching process. Such potential social reinforcement suppliers as teachers, parents, and friends may be either nonrewarding or simply unavailable. However, if children can be helped to become their own reinforcement suppliers, if they can be shown how to evaluate their own skill behaviors and reward or approve their own effective performance, they will have made a major stride toward increasing the chances that their newly learned skills will be performed in a reliable and lasting manner in real-life settings. Clearly, this is the goal of any reinforcement program. However, until the child has the skills and self-confidence to evaluate his own performance, others (teachers, parents, peers) must be the reinforcement providers.

Reinforcement Enhancers

The effectiveness of reinforcement in influencing performance will depend on several characteristics of the reinforcement used. These characteristics include the following.

Type of reinforcement

McGehee and Thayer (1961) have observed that "what one person regards as a rewarding experience may be regarded by another as neutral or nonrewarding, or even punishing" (p. 140). Although it is true that certain types of reinforcers (e.g., approval, food, affection, and money) have a high likelihood of serving as effective reinforcers for most children most of the time, this will not always be the case. Both the children's own reinforcement history and current needs will affect whether the intended reinforcer is, in fact, reinforcing. Teaching procedures will optimally take these individualizing considerations into account. This means not only choosing between given material, social, and self-reinforcers when necessary, but also making changes in these choices in a continuing and sensitive manner.

Delay of reinforcement

Research on learning has shown consistently that behavior change occurs most effectively when the reinforcement follows immediately after the desired behavior. Reinforcement strengthens the behavior that was occurring just before the reinforcement took place and makes it likely that the particular behavior will occur again. Thus, delayed reinforcement may lead to the strengthening of inappropriate or ineffective behaviors if these behaviors occur between the desired behavior and the onset of reinforcement.

Response-contingent reinforcement

It is necessary that the child see and understand a relationship between the behavior she is exhibiting and the reinforcement that occurs. Delivering the reinforcement conditionally upon the behavior and, further, making it sufficiently clear to the child that the reinforcement is contingent upon this selected behavior are vital in creating the linkage between performance and reinforcement.

Amount and quality of reinforcement

The amount and quality of reinforcement also determine a child's performance. With certain important exceptions, the greater the amount of reinforcement, the greater the positive effect upon performance. One limitation of this principle is that increases in certain types of reinforcement do increase performance, but in smaller and smaller increments. Research on the amount of reinforcement indicates that, in the laboratory at least, subjects do not appear to learn (acquire new knowledge) more rapidly for large rewards than for small ones. Once learning has taken place, however, performance will often be more dependable if larger rewards are given.

Opportunity for reinforcement

An additional requirement for successful and consistent performance is that the behavior to be reinforced occur with sufficient frequency for reinforcement to be provided often enough. If behaviors are too infrequent, insufficient opportunity will exist to influence their occurrence through contingent reinforcement. Role playing provides excellent opportunities to reinforce the behaviors desired.

Partial or intermittent reinforcement

Partial reinforcement refers to the reinforcement of only some of the child's correct responses by reinforcing at fixed times (e.g., at the end of each activity period), at a fixed number of responses (e.g., every third correct response), on a variable time or response schedule (e.g., randomly choosing, within limits, the time or correct response to reward), and on other types of schedules. In all instances it has been consistently shown that behaviors that have been intermittently reinforced last longer than behaviors reinforced each time they occur. An optimal reinforcement schedule provides rewards for all desired responses initially, thinning to one or another type of partial reinforcement schedule as the desired behavior continues.

The following points serve to summarize performance feedback by reinforcement:

1. The reinforcement must be seen as rewarding by the child.

2. The reinforcement should be given immediately after the desired behavior.

3. The child must make the connection between the behavior he exhibits and the reinforcement he receives.

4. In general, the greater the amount of reinforcement, the greater the positive effect on performance.

5. The desirable behavior must occur with sufficient frequency for the reinforcement to be provided often enough.

6. Reinforcement should be given on a rich schedule at first, then thinned to an intermittent schedule.

In other words, research evidence indicates that high levels of performance are likely to occur if the child is given enough opportunity to receive immediate reinforcement of a kind that is right for him, in sufficiently large amounts, offered in a response-contingent manner on an intermittent schedule.

Considerable evidence supports the impact on behavior change of modeling, role playing, and performance feedback in the form of social reinforcement. As noted earlier, neither modeling nor role playing alone yields results nearly as effective as the two combined. A similar situation exists with reinforcement. Although it is true that reinforcement alone is more likely to lead to lasting behavior change than either modeling or role playing alone, it is also true that the behaviors to be reinforced must occur with sufficient correctness and frequency for reinforcement to have its intended effect. The addition of modeling provides a higher frequency of the desired behaviors and thus increases the likelihood that the behaviors to be reinforced will be correct. The final Skillstreaming component is responsive to the ultimate purpose of any learning endeavor – transfer of what has been learned from the teaching setting to the classroom or other real-life settings.

TRANSFER TRAINING

The main interest of any teaching program, and where most teaching programs fail, is not in children's performance during the training activity, but instead in how well they perform in their real lives. If skills have been satisfactorily performed at the time of teaching, what procedures are available to maximize the chances that such performance will consistently continue in school, at home, or in other places or situations where skill use is appropriate? In other words, how can transfer of training be encouraged?

Transfer Training Enhancers

Research has identified a number of principles of transfer enhancement. Attending to all these principles greatly increases the likelihood of successful transfer. These principles will be described in the rest of this chapter, and their incorporation into Skillstreaming will be examined in subsequent chapters. Transfer and maintenance of learned behaviors may be enhanced by (1) the teaching setting, materials, and personnel; (2) reinforcement systems; and (3) task instruction.

Teaching setting, materials, and personnel

Generalization or transfer is facilitated when the setting in which the teaching occurs closely resembles the natural setting where the skill will be used. It has been demonstrated repeatedly that the greater the number of *identical elements,* or characteristics shared by the teaching and application settings, the greater the later transfer from teaching to real life. Ideally, both the interpersonal and physical characteristics of the teaching and application settings would be similar in as many ways as possible. Thus, if possible, the children would be instructed along with others with whom they interact regularly. Also, the teaching would take place to the extent feasible in school and home settings or in other real-life environments in which the children actually interact, rather than at an instructional center or psychologist/counselor's office. When this is not possible and simulation must be used in lieu of teaching in the natural environment, the physical setting (i.e., furnishings, materials) should be as much like the natural setting as possible (Buckley & Walker, 1978). Using props and arranging the teaching environment to resemble the real-life environment where the skill should be performed will likely enhance transfer.

The actual use of a skill is facilitated by teaching the skill in a *variety of settings* and in response to a variety of persons (Stokes & Baer, 1977; Stokes, Baer, & Jackson, 1974). Several researchers have demonstrated that transfer is greater when a variety of such teaching stimuli are employed (Callantine & Warren, 1955; Duncan, 1958; Shore & Sechrest, 1961). The use in Skillstreaming of several different school settings, models, teachers, and role-playing coactors is based on this principle of transfer enhancement.

An additional method of facilitating transfer focuses on *changes in the environment* that will support new behavior (Walker, 1979). The needs of children are all too likely to be forgotten once they leave the teaching environment for real-life settings. Teaching provides skills, information, knowledge, and the potential for successful application. However, it is primarily real-life reinforcement – by teachers, parents, peers, and the children themselves – that will determine whether the learning will endure. Homework assignments are a major vehicle for presenting opportunities for real-life experience and reinforcement. The nature and format of such assignments will be discussed in chapter 5.

Reinforcement systems

The importance of continued, intermittent reinforcement for lasting behavior change should be stressed. Are the new behaviors ignored? Or, as is perhaps more common, are they reinforced at first and then ignored? Continued reinforcement, though gradually thinned or made more intermittent, is clearly a necessary part of enduring transfer training. When implementing a Skillstreaming program for skill-deficient children, the teacher should help parents, principals, other teachers and school personnel, and peers understand how to provide continued real-life reinforcement. Such reinforcement must take into account all the dimensions discussed earlier as critical aspects of the performance feedback process (scheduling, nature, amount, etc.). Using reinforcers during Skillstreaming that may also occur naturally in the environment, such as a smile and a pleasant thank you, will increase the chance that children will be responsive to reinforcement by others outside of the teaching setting (Stokes & Baer, 1977).

Task instruction

It has been well established that practiced behavior, or behavior that has occurred frequently in the past, will be more likely to occur in future situations. This principle originates from research on *overlearning*, or the notion that the higher the degree of original learning, the greater the probability of later transfer. In the context of Skillstreaming, this means that the greater the number of correct enactments of a given skill during role playing, the more likely it is that the skill will transfer. In addition to increasing the likelihood of positive transfer, overlearning may also decrease the chances that negative transfer (interference rather than facilitation) will occur. When more than one skill is being taught, negative transfer or interference with learning is likely to occur if instruction on the second skill is begun while the first is still only partially learned. This is less likely to occur when the correct skill behavior is practiced enough to ensure that overlearning has occurred.

Even though a child has learned a skill well in the Skillstreaming setting, it is desirable for transfer-enhancement purposes that the instruction be withdrawn systematically rather than stopped abruptly (Buckley & Walker, 1978). Periodic review of the learned skills (booster sessions) will assist with such systematic fading of instruction.

Describing the specific types of situations in the real world in which children should use a given skill is called *instructed generalization* (Stokes & Baer, 1977). The children can thus be encouraged to use a particular skill in a variety of natural problematic situations and real-life settings. Historically, teachers and parents have used this principle of generalization by instructing children during the "teachable moment," or when the skill is actually needed. Thus, giving reminders or instructions when the need arises is an easily implemented and valuable principle to enhance transfer.

SUMMARY

Four procedures for teaching prosocial skills—modeling, role playing, performance feedback, and transfer training—have been examined. The nature of each, the techniques that maximize their effectiveness, and samples of supporting research have been presented. In discussing each of these procedures, we raised one or more notes of caution. For example, although modeling does result in the learning of new behaviors, without sufficient practice, old behaviors tend to reoccur. Practice or role playing is also an important aid to new learning, but the behaviors practiced must be the correct ones, a situation made more likely when the behaviors are illustrated by prior modeling. Given both modeling and role playing, the newly learned behaviors are more likely to persist. Yet this will not occur unless the child sees the use of these behaviors as a rewarding experience—hence the necessity for reinforcement. Also, the behaviors must be performed by the child correctly and with sufficient frequency to ensure that reinforcement occurs often enough. Without sufficient frequency, the new behaviors, even if reinforced, may not be learned. Procedures such as modeling and role playing can lead to sufficient frequency of correct performance. Combining these three procedures provides a much more effective approach to skill instruction. Yet a truly effective approach must also demonstrate learning beyond the teaching setting. Thus, we presented several principles to enhance the likelihood that skills learned in the teaching environment will transfer to the child's real-life setting.

CHAPTER 3

Identifying and Evaluating Children for Skillstreaming

This chapter describes techniques to help teachers create a Skillstreaming plan tailored to the individual skill assets and deficits of each child. By applying the methods presented, the teacher, with the help of other school personnel and significant individuals in the child's environment, will be able to identify the children most in need of such training, assess their skill strengths and weaknesses, assign them to specific Skillstreaming groups, and evaluate their progress in learning prosocial behaviors. The chapter additionally includes several useful measures and forms for identifying children's skill deficits and for evaluating their response to Skillstreaming instruction.

OVERVIEW OF ASSESSMENT ISSUES

Two primary problems relating to the assessment of a child's social functioning currently exist (Cartledge & Milburn, 1980). First, as is assumed by a social learning perspective (Bandura, 1977), people learn many behaviors from observing the actions of others. A child may therefore possess a cognitive understanding of socially acceptable behaviors but may be unable to translate this social knowledge into action. Thus, it becomes necessary to assess both the child's *knowledge* of social responses and her *ability* to perform these behaviors under appropriate circumstances. Second, because views vary widely about what is considered appropriate and acceptable in children's social behavior, reliability among the different persons who rate the child (adults, peers, even the child herself) may pose a problem.

Assessing social skills deficits requires an understanding of the situational parameters of the behavior (time and place), the antecedents to the behavior (the behavior of others prior to the occurrence of the behavior), and the positive and negative consequences following the behavior (peer and adult reactions; Foster & Ritchey, 1979). For example, the behavior of shouting may be appropriate within a given context (e.g., on the playground or at a baseball game) but inappropriate in a different setting (e.g., in the classroom or hallways). Certain types of aggression (i.e., provoked aggression) have actually been found to correlate positively with peer popularity (Hartup, 1970; Lesser, 1959). Quilitch and Risley (1973) additionally found that the rates of social interaction among preschoolers were higher when social toys were presented than when the children were given nonsocial toys. The social interaction of children has also been found to be affected by the physical structure of the environment – specifically, the availability of space (Alevizos, Labrecque, & Gregersen, 1972) and the degree of adult imposed structure (Greenwood, Walker, Todd, & Hops, 1978).

Because many behaviors are specific to a given situation, the consistency of a child's skill deficits is a further issue of concern. One way of alleviating some of the problems associated with this concern is to apply assessment procedures to a variety of social situations (e.g., the playground, cafeteria, hallways), during various structured school settings (e.g., different classroom activities), and in response to different individuals (e.g., peers, teachers, parents). Conducting repeated measures over time will also help.

ASSESSMENT METHODS

The assessment of children's social functioning should rely on a variety of substantiated assessment techniques. The following paragraphs examine sociometrics, naturalistic observation, analogue observation, behavior rating scales, and self-reports.

Sociometrics

Children who demonstrate deficits in prosocial skill use are very likely to be those who lack acceptance by their peers (Barclay, 1966). Sociometric techniques use peer judgments to identify children who are accepted, rejected, neglected, or controversial (Coie, Dodge, & Coppotelli, 1982). Such techniques are often criticized for their intrusiveness (O'Leary & Johnson, 1979), but the information gained from them is a useful predictor of later socioemotional adjustment (Rolf, 1976; Kupersmidt, 1983). Sociometrics are, along with naturalistic observation and teacher rating scales, quite commonly applied in research on social functioning (Gresham, 1981). Together, these three measures have been used to evaluate the social withdrawal of preschoolers (Greenwood, Walker, & Hops, 1977) and the social status of aggressive and aggressive/withdrawn boys (Milich & Landau, 1982).

Classroom sociometrics generally have good psychometric properties (Milich & Landau, 1982), including good reliability across instruments (Marshall & McCandless, 1957), sources (Walker, 1967; Weir, Stevenson, & Graham, 1980), and time (Asher, Singleton, Tinsley, & Hymel, 1979), as well as good predictive validity (Gronlund & Anderson, 1957; Hartup, Glazer, & Charlesworth, 1967; Hymel & Asher, 1977). It should be noted that the majority of data used to establish reliability and validity of sociometrics have been collected from preschoolers.

Positive correlations have also been found between teacher ratings and sociometric ratings (Gronlund, 1951; Roff, Sells, & Golden, 1972), although such correlations have their limits. Specifically, teachers and peers have been found to differ in their agreement on the tolerability of behaviors such as aggression (Lesser, 1959). Peery (1979) also found that teachers ranked amiable and isolated children differently than did peers. As pointed out by Kohlberg, LaCrosse, and Ricks (1972), children may be sensitive to behavioral differences that may not easily be perceived by adults.

Although sociometric devices provide reliable information about children's social impact on their peer groups, they indicate very little about the specific skills or behaviors children exhibit with their peers (Dodge, 1985; Putallaz & Gottman, 1981). Sociometric techniques also tend to be situation-specific (Gresham, 1982) and should be supported by other data, such as teacher ratings and behavioral observations. Even with these disadvantages, sociometric techniques have been found useful both for screening socially incompetent children and for socially validating changes in behavior measured in a more direct manner (e.g., by naturalistic observation; Foster & Ritchey, 1979). A variety of sociometric techniques exist; among the most common are peer nomination and roster rating scales.

Peer nomination

The peer nomination method, originated by Moreno (1934), requires youngsters to name peers according to selected criteria. For example, children may be asked to name the boys or girls with whom they most like to play or work (Peery, 1979). Most often, they are asked to nominate three peers for each category. Because there appears to be a sex bias in sociometric ratings (Singleton & Asher, 1977), children should be requested to nominate only peers of the same sex. The higher the number of positive choices, the greater the indication of peer acceptance. Conversely, the higher the number of negative choices, the greater the indication of peer rejection (Asher & Taylor, 1982).

When using the peer nomination method, children should make both positive and negative nominations. If only positive nominations are requested, then a child who receives none may erroneously be assumed to be rejected. This child may actually be neglected (not really considered by peers, but not rejected) or noncontroversial (generally liked, but not a "best friend"; Asher & Taylor, 1982). It must also be mentioned that the number of nominations received for each child largely depends on the number of peers making the nominations; therefore, when this technique is employed with a small group of children, the number of nominations should be proportioned to the total group size (Kane & Lawler, 1978).

McCandless and Marshall (1957) developed a peer nomination technique applicable to prereading children. In this method, each child is individually presented with photographs of all class members and asked (1) who the child's best friend is, (2) with whom the child would most like to play, and (3) with whom the child would most like to work. The child then points to a classmate's photograph to indicate the nomination in each category.

Roster rating scales

Whereas peer nominations are employed primarily to indicate social status (e.g., friendship), roster rating scales are used to provide information about specific behavioral aspects that may contribute to a youngster's popularity or rejection. In this method, each child is given a list or roster of all classmates and then is asked to rate each classmate on a Likert-type scale (for prereaders, a three-point scale anchored by smiling, neutral, and frowning faces) according to specific questions (Foster & Ritchey, 1979). Such questions might typically include "How much do you like to play (or work) with this person?" or "Whom would you most like to sit next to?" The questions can be varied to assess different types of behaviors (e.g., how much the person helps others or how often the person starts fights).

One advantage of the roster rating scale method over that of peer nomination is that every child receives a rating from every peer. For instance, Hymel and Asher (1977) found that whereas many children received no nominations on a positive peer measure, they received relatively high scores on a rating scale measure, suggesting that although these youngsters had no best friends in the class, they were generally liked by their classmates. The roster rating scale method further avoids the difficulty of various group sizes inherent in peer nominations (Foster & Ritchey, 1979) and has superior test-retest reliability (Oden & Asher, 1977).

Naturalistic Observation

Given that interaction among people consists of observable verbal, paralinguistic, and motor behaviors, naturalistic observation is a logical strategy to assess social functioning (Hops, 1982). In the process of naturalistic observation (sometimes called *direct observation*), the teacher watches what the youngster does at particular times or in specific situations. This information is then coded and reported in relevant categories of behavior, such as positive or negative peer interaction or number of questions asked in class. Such observations might involve taking frequency counts (e.g., of a child's joining in games or responding to peers' overtures to play), recording duration (e.g., the length of time a child spends crying or playing appropriately with peers), or making anecdotal records (e.g., of specific behaviors of concern and the antecedents and consequences of those behaviors). Another system includes time sampling observations, which give information not only about the target child's prosocial behavior, but also about the behavior of peers in the same setting (Greenwood, Walker, Todd, & Hops, 1979; Hops et al., 1978).

Naturalistic observation has been used to assess children's social withdrawal (Cooke & Apolloni, 1976; Strain, 1977), sharing behavior (Rogers-Warren & Baer, 1976), aggressiveness (Forehand & King, 1977), disruptions (Iwata & Bailey, 1974), and cooperative play (Kirby & Toler, 1970). One major advantage of employing naturalistic observation is that the antecedents and consequences of particular behaviors can be identified (Gresham, 1982). Observation techniques also lend themselves to repeated measurements, thus allowing evaluators to establish trends in youngsters' social behavior patterns (Gresham, 1982).

Some studies have suggested that children's observed rates of interaction do not correlate with social status as measured by sociometric techniques (Foster & Ritchey, 1983; Gottman, 1977; Jennings, 1975; Krantz, 1982). Other investigators (Hartup, Glazer, & Charlesworth, 1967) have found a positive correlation between positive peer interaction and sociometric acceptance, and between negative peer interaction and sociometric rejection. Such correlations have been more consistent for the preschool child than for those of school age (Asher & Hymel, 1981). As these differences suggest, both quantitative and qualitative behavioral categories need to be selected for observation. It must also be noted that, although one can observe social behaviors in a particular situation, these same behaviors are not always demonstrated in other situations or settings; thus, several observations across a variety of school settings will yield the most accurate and useful information. Finally, to minimize the possibility of inferences being drawn about the data, observational codes should include specific behaviors (e.g., hitting a peer) rather than global categories (e.g., aggression).

Analogue Observation

An alternative to naturalistic observation is analogue observation, which involves conducting simulation activities in which certain aspects of the natural environment are staged and the child's prosocial skill proficiency and deficiency are then observed. For instance, instead of attempting to observe actual interactions between a child and a teasing peer, one could construct a simulation in the form of a role-playing task in which the child must react to teasing.

The role-played interaction is less time consuming and easier to observe and record in a standardized manner than a similar real-life interaction. However, there does not appear to be a strong relationship between social behavior shown in simulated situations and social behavior in real life (Gresham, 1983; Matson, Rotatori, & Helsel, 1983; Van Hasselt, Bellack, & Hersen, 1979; Van Hasselt, Hersen, & Bellack, 1981). For this reason, analogue observations may be more useful in evaluating a child's social knowledge (Spivack, Platt, & Shure, 1976) than in evaluating his actual social behavior.

Behavior Rating Scales

Another way of identifying skill deficient children is to use behavior rating scales (Greenwood et al., 1977). In this method, historically used to identify children with a range of problems (Walker et al., 1983), an observer who has had an opportunity to watch the child on an ongoing basis is given a list of behaviors and asked to rate them according to intensity, frequency, or other criteria. A variety of individuals—parents, teachers, or other school personnel—may evaluate the child's behavior using this method. Thus, useful information can be gathered from several sources without necessarily involving the child directly. Examples of some behavior rating scales designed for use with young children include the Social Behavior Assessment (Stephens, 1978, 1980); the Social Competence Scale (Kohn & Rosman, 1972); and the Matson Evaluation of Social Skills with Youngsters (Matson et al., 1983).

The results of numerous studies suggest that teacher ratings of behavior distinguish between average children and those who exhibit learning and behavior problems (Behar, 1977; Campbell, 1974; McCarthy & Paraskevopoulos, 1969; Swift & Spivack, 1969). Teacher ratings are also felt to be useful in predicting the popularity of preschool children (Connolly & Doyle, 1981) and later overall social adjustment (Janes & Hesselbrock, 1978; Janes, Hesselbrock, Myers, & Penniman, 1979). Although teacher ratings may be affected by such characteristics as the child's academic ability, family background, and certain personality traits (Weir et al., 1980), these ratings have shown good validity when compared with other measures. Furthermore, behavior rating scales allow one to gather information about a child's skill strengths and weaknesses relatively unobtrusively and, because the information gained is based on extensive observations of the child, it can reflect enduring behavioral characteristics (Asher & Taylor, 1982).

Reports from the child's parents and/or other adults who have a history of involvement with the child can also be a valuable aid in assessing the child's skill deficits. Because we know that behavior may vary from one setting to the next, the person or persons evaluating the child should have knowledge of the child's social behavior in environments such as the home and neighborhood. Such information will help in determining the consistency of the child's behavioral skills and further dictate specific skill areas to be addressed in Skillstreaming instruction. Parent rating scales such as the Connors Parent Rating Scale (Connors, 1975) and the Behavioral Rating Profile (Brown & Hammill, 1978) may additionally be helpful as part of this assessment process.

One particular kind of behavior rating scale is the social skills inventory, in which the items to be rated are skill behaviors. The Teacher Skill Checklist (Figure 1, p. 30) and the Parent Skill Checklist (Figure 2, p. 34) are examples of social skills inventories. These measures can be used to help evaluate and group children for Skillstreaming instruction. Because these inventories are adaptations of measures used with other age populations (and thus not standardized or norm-referenced), their use should be limited to pretesting and posttesting associated directly with intervention.

Self-Reports

The direct involvement of young children in the assessment process has been accomplished most frequently by interviewing them regarding possible solutions to hypothetical social dilemmas. Peery (1979), for example, asked preschoolers to interpret affective cues presented in short story vignettes, and Gouze, Gordon, and Rayias (1983) used a series of cartoons to assess a preschooler's recall of social information. Both quantitative and qualitative differences in young children's solutions to such dilemmas have been found to distinguish among varying degrees of peer acceptance and social adjustment (Shure & Spivack, 1980; Spivack & Shure, 1974). Another reason for including children's self-reports is that the effectiveness of skills training may be affected by the value of peer interaction held by those children (Evers-Pasquale, 1978; Evers-Pasquale & Sherman, 1975). Stated otherwise, the youngsters' own appraisals of skill competency may provide not only assessment and group placement information, but also valuable motivational data.

Children's felt needs or experienced deficits may be of great use in selecting skills that participating children are willing and even eager to learn. Two such measures are included here: the Child Skill Checklist

(Figure 3, p. 41), designed to assess youngsters' perceptions of their own social skills, and the Skill Situations Measure (Figure 5, p. 46), designed to assess children's social knowledge.

ASSESSMENT MEASURES AND FORMS

Teacher Skill Checklist

The Teacher Skill Checklist (Figure 1, p. 30), designed to be completed by a teacher or other adult familiar with the child's behaviors in a variety of situations, requires the rater to indicate the frequency with which a child uses each of the 40 skills taught in the Skillstreaming group. This criterion-referenced measure is intended to be used as part of an assessment battery to screen a child's skill strengths and weaknesses, as a guide for specific skill instruction in a classroom setting, and as one measure of the progress the child has made in acquiring prosocial skills.

Parent Skill Checklist

The Parent Skill Checklist (Figure 2, p. 34) is designed to be completed by the child's parent in an attempt to assess the parent's perceptions of the child's prosocial behaviors in the home and neighborhood environments. Like the Teacher Skill Checklist, this measure allows the parent to respond to descriptions of the 40 prosocial skills in terms of the frequency of skill use. Even though information relative to the child's skill use outside of the school setting may be very useful, some discretion in requesting a parent to complete this checklist is in order. The complete checklist may be given, or specific questions on the checklist may be selected to assess the child's strengths and weaknesses in skill areas that are of concern in the school setting. Others may wish to use the checklist with parents in an interview format.

Child Skill Checklist

The Child Skill Checklist (Figure 3, p. 41) is designed to assess the children's own perceptions of the skills they feel they want or need to learn. Most appropriate for children ages 5 and 6, the checklist is designed to be read to the individual child or to small groups of children in four separate evaluation sessions.

During each of these evaluation sessions, the teacher helps the children mark the Child Skill Response Record (Figure 4, p. 45) to indicate their answers. Directions would involve something like the following statement:

I will read you some questions that I want you to answer as best you can. There are no right or wrong answers—I want you to answer the way you really feel. After you hear the question, if your answer is "Yes, most of the time," then color the happy face [teacher demonstrates]. If your answer to the question is "Sometimes," then color the plain face [teacher demonstrates]. If your answer is "Not very often," then color the sad face [teacher demonstrates]. Be sure to ask if there is anything you don't understand.

The teacher then asks children to put a finger on the picture corresponding to the question (rabbit, teddy bear, cat, etc.), listen carefully to the question, then color the face that shows how they feel. After the children have colored in the appropriate face, the teacher then directs them to place a finger on the picture corresponding to the next question, and so on. Each question should be repeated at least one time.

Prior to the administration of this instrument, the teacher should be sure that each child has a good understanding of the vocabulary included in the checklist (e.g., *directions, bored, ignore*). It may be necessary to discuss the meaning of terms prior to the administration of the checklist or to define terms as they come up. In any event, the children should be well oriented to the preschool or kindergarten setting prior to using this measure.

Skill Situations Measure

The Skill Situations Measure (Figure 5, p. 46) is intended to assess the youngster's knowledge of the 40 prosocial skills when presented with situations suggesting their use. In this measure, the child is read a brief problematic situation and is asked to respond either verbally or by demonstrating a solution to the problem. The child's response is then recorded on the Skill Situations Response Record (Figure 6, p. 50). Materials helpful in administering this assessment include puppets, crayons, markers, drawing paper, a toy car, a board game such as Candy Land, and a few toy dishes. Directions would involve something like the following statement:

I'm going to tell you some little stories about Opie the Opossum and Lila the Lamb. I want you to tell me, or show me, what either Opie or Lila would do with these problems.

This technique will be most useful in assessing the child's knowledge of ways to deal with situations in which some deficit has already been observed. Therefore, the teacher may choose to select the most pertinent situations instead of administering the measure in its entirety. It is important to emphasize that knowledge displayed in response to these situations does not necessarily translate into real-life skill performance. Verbalizing or demonstrating a prosocial response in the assessment setting suggests only that the child has an awareness of prosocial actions related to that situation. If other assessments (e.g., Teacher and/or Parent Skill Checklists) indicate that the child does not actually use the prosocial skill, then it will be necessary for the child to be taught that skill directly. If the child verbalizes or demonstrates an aggressive or withdrawn response, this may suggest that the child will need to see the skill modeled in numerous situations prior to being asked to act out that skill in a role-play setting.

Skills Grouping Chart

Information from the Teacher and Parent Skill Checklists may be used to group children on the basis of shared skill deficiencies. The youngsters' names and ratings on each skill are entered on the Skills Grouping Chart (Figure 7, p. 59), thus providing a visual summary of ratings of individual strengths and weaknesses in all skills. By listing both teacher and parent ratings on each skill, the teacher can easily note where discrepancies between ratings exist. In some cases, the child's responses on the Child Skill Checklist may be used in addition to or in lieu of parent responses. The teacher should scan the charts for low ratings (e.g., 1s or 2s on either checklist) within the same skill category and then, if possible, assign youngsters with similar patterns accordingly.

In instances where the class as a whole will participate in Skillstreaming, a greater range of skill proficiencies and deficiencies will likely be apparent. In this case, entering the teacher and parent ratings for each student onto the Skills Grouping Chart will provide a profile of the entire class. The teacher then has the option of selecting those skills in which many class members are deficient.

Progress Summary Sheet

The teacher may use the Progress Summary Sheet (Figure 8, p. 61) to record each child's skill level, as noted on the Teacher Skill Checklist, before and after participation in Skillstreaming. This method provides a record of the progress the child has made in each of the skills taught.

Teacher Record

The Teacher Record (Figure 9, p. 63) defines the behavioral goals or objectives relevant to a particular child. Teachers, counselors, school psychologists, and others are required in many cases, especially when working with special education students, to define individual behavioral objectives and then to evaluate the degree to which those objectives are reached. Such definition and evaluation of objectives can be accomplished in Skill-streaming by planning which skills will be taught and using the Teacher Record to describe the child's progress.

SUMMARY

A combination of the assessment techniques discussed in this chapter (sociometrics, naturalistic observation, analogue observation, behavior rating scales, and self-reports) will provide a comprehensive picture of the children's areas of skill deficits and strengths, as well as useful information for planning and evaluating the success of a prosocial skills training effort. However, it is not necessary, nor is it practical, to complete all of these assessment procedures for every participating child. Instead, these procedures are intended to reflect the range of assessment instruments from which an appropriate measurement battery should be selected for a given youngster or group.

FIGURE 1 Teacher Skill Checklist

Name _____ Birth Date _____

School/Program _____

Teacher/Evaluator _____ Assessment Date _____

Directions: Based on your observations in various situations, rate each child's use of the following skills.

Circle 1 if the child *almost never* uses the skill.
Circle 2 if the child *seldom* uses the skill.
Circle 3 if the child *sometimes* uses the skill.
Circle 4 if the child *often* uses the skill.
Circle 5 if the child *almost always* uses the skill.

	Almost never	Seldom	Sometimes	Often	Almost always
1. Does the child appear to listen when others are speaking and seem to understand what is said?	1	2	3	4	5
2. Does the child speak to others in a friendly manner?	1	2	3	4	5
3. Does the child use a brave or assertive tone of voice in a conflict with another child?	1	2	3	4	5
4. Does the child say thank you or in another way let others know he/she appreciates help given, favors, and so forth?	1	2	3	4	5
5. Does the child say when he/she has done a good job?	1	2	3	4	5
6. Does the child request help when needed in an acceptable manner?	1	2	3	4	5

	Almost never	Seldom	Sometimes	Often	Almost always

7. Does the child ask favors of others in an acceptable way?   1 2 3 4 5

8. Does the child ignore other children or situations when it is desirable to do so?   1 2 3 4 5

9. Does the child ask questions about something he/she doesn't understand?   1 2 3 4 5

10. Does the child seem to understand directions and follow them?   1 2 3 4 5

11. Does the child continue to try when something is difficult instead of giving up?   1 2 3 4 5

12. Does the child interrupt when necessary in an appropriate manner?   1 2 3 4 5

13. Does the child acknowledge acquaintances when it is appropriate to do so?   1 2 3 4 5

14. Does the child pay attention to a person's nonverbal language and seem to understand what is being communicated?   1 2 3 4 5

15. Does the child use acceptable ways of joining in an ongoing activity or group?   1 2 3 4 5

16. Does the child wait his/her turn when playing a game with others?   1 2 3 4 5

17. Does the child share most materials and toys with peers?   1 2 3 4 5

18. Does the child recognize when someone needs or wants help and offer assistance?   1 2 3 4 5

FIGURE 1   Teacher Skill Checklist (cont'd)

	Almost never	Seldom	Sometimes	Often	Almost always
19. Does the child ask other children to play or extend an invitation to others to join in his/her activity?	1	2	3	4	5
20. Does the child play games with peers in a fair manner?	1	2	3	4	5
21. Does the child identify his/her feelings?	1	2	3	4	5
22. Does the child deal with being left out of an activity without losing control or becoming upset?	1	2	3	4	5
23. Does the child verbally express when he/she seems upset?	1	2	3	4	5
24. When afraid, does the child know why he/she is afraid and deal with this fear in an acceptable way (e.g., by talking about it)?	1	2	3	4	5
25. Does the child identify how another person appears to be feeling by what the person says?	1	2	3	4	5
26. Does the child show that he/she likes someone in an acceptable way?	1	2	3	4	5
27. Does the child deal with being teased in acceptable ways?	1	2	3	4	5
28. Does the child use acceptable ways to express his/her anger?	1	2	3	4	5
29. Does the child accurately assess what is fair and unfair?	1	2	3	4	5

30. When a problem occurs, does the child state alternative, prosocial ways to solve the problem?   1 2 3 4 5

31. Does the child accept the consequences for his/her behavior without becoming angry or upset?   1 2 3 4 5

32. Is the child able to relax when tense or upset?   1 2 3 4 5

33. Does the child accept making mistakes without becoming upset?   1 2 3 4 5

34. Is the child honest when confronted with a negative behavior?   1 2 3 4 5

35. Does the child refrain from telling on others about small problems?   1 2 3 4 5

36. Does the child accept losing at a game or activity without becoming upset or angry?   1 2 3 4 5

37. Does the child accept not being first at a game or activity?   1 2 3 4 5

38. Does the child say no in an acceptable manner to things he/she doesn't want to do or to things that may get him/her into trouble?   1 2 3 4 5

39. Does the child accept being told no without becoming upset?   1 2 3 4 5

40. Does the child choose acceptable activities on his/her own when feeling bored?   1 2 3 4 5

FIGURE 2 Parent Skill Checklist

Name _____ Date _____

Child's Name _____ Birth Date _____

Directions: Based on your observations in various situations, rate
your child's use of the following skills.

Circle 1 if the child *almost never* uses the skill.
Circle 2 if the child *seldom* uses the skill.
Circle 3 if the child *sometimes* uses the skill.
Circle 4 if the child *often* uses the skill.
Circle 5 if the child *almost always* uses the skill.

	Almost never	Seldom	Sometimes	Often	Almost always
1. Does your child listen and understand when you or others talk to him/her?	1	2	3	4	5
Comments:					
2. Does your child speak to others in a friendly manner?	1	2	3	4	5
Comments:					
3. Does your child use a brave or assertive manner when in a conflict with another child?	1	2	3	4	5
Comments:					
4. Does your child say thank you or in another way show thanks when someone does something nice for him/her?	1	2	3	4	5
Comments:					

	Almost never	Seldom	Sometimes	Often	Almost always

5. Does your child tell you when he/she has done a good job?   1 2 3 4 5

Comments:

6. Does your child ask in a friendly way when he/she needs help?   1 2 3 4 5

Comments:

7. Does your child ask favors of others in an acceptable way?   1 2 3 4 5

Comments:

8. Does your child ignore other children or situations when it is desirable to ignore them?   1 2 3 4 5

Comments:

9. Does your child ask questions about something he/she doesn't understand?   1 2 3 4 5

Comments:

10. Does your child seem to understand and follow directions you give?   1 2 3 4 5

Comments:

11. Does your child continue to try when something is difficult instead of giving up?   1 2 3 4 5

Comments:

35

FIGURE 2 Parent Skill Checklist (cont'd)

	Almost never	Seldom	Sometimes	Often	Almost always

12. Does your child know when and how to interrupt when he/she needs or wants something?   1 2 3 4 5

Comments:

13. Does your child acknowledge acquaintances when it is appropriate to do so?   1 2 3 4 5

Comments:

14. Does your child pay attention to a person's nonverbal language and seem to understand what is being communicated?   1 2 3 4 5

Comments:

15. Does your child know acceptable ways of joining in an activity with friends or family?   1 2 3 4 5

Comments:

16. Does your child wait his/her turn when playing a game with others?   1 2 3 4 5

Comments:

17. Does your child share most materials and toys with his/her friends?   1 2 3 4 5

Comments:

	Almost never	Seldom	Sometimes	Often	Almost always

18. Does your child recognize when someone needs or wants help and offer this help?   1   2   3   4   5

    Comments:

19. Does your child ask other children to play or join in his/her activity?   1   2   3   4   5

    Comments:

20. Does your child play games with friends in a fair manner?   1   2   3   4   5

    Comments:

21. Does your child identify his/her feelings?   1   2   3   4   5

    Comments:

22. Does your child deal with being left out of an activity without losing control or becoming upset?   1   2   3   4   5

    Comments:

23. Does your child talk about his/her problems when upset?   1   2   3   4   5

    Comments:

FIGURE 2 Parent Skill Checklist (cont'd)

	Almost never	Seldom	Sometimes	Often	Almost always
24. Does your child know why he/she is afraid and deal with this fear in an acceptable way (e.g., by talking about it)?	1	2	3	4	5

Comments:

25. Does your child identify how another person seems to be feeling by what the person says?	1	2	3	4	5

Comments:

26. Does your child show that he/she likes someone in an acceptable way?	1	2	3	4	5

Comments:

27. Does your child deal with being teased in acceptable ways?	1	2	3	4	5

Comments:

28. Does your child use acceptable ways to express his/her anger?	1	2	3	4	5

Comments:

29. Does your child accurately assess what is fair and unfair?	1	2	3	4	5

Comments:

30. When a problem occurs, does your child   1   2   3   4   5
offer alternative, acceptable ways to solve
the problem?

Comments:

31. Does your child accept the consequences   1   2   3   4   5
of his/her behavior without becoming angry
or upset?

Comments:

32. Is your child able to relax when tense or   1   2   3   4   5
upset?

Comments:

33. Does your child accept making mistakes   1   2   3   4   5
without becoming upset?

Comments:

34. Does your child admit that he/she has   1   2   3   4   5
done something wrong when confronted?

Comments:

35. Does your child refrain from telling on   1   2   3   4   5
others about small problems?

Comments:

FIGURE 2 Parent Skill Checklist (cont'd)

	Almost never	Seldom	Sometimes	Often	Almost always
36. Does your child accept losing at a game without becoming upset or angry?	1	2	3	4	5

Comments:

37. Does your child accept not being first at a game or activity?	1	2	3	4	5

Comments:

38. Does your child say no in an acceptable way to things he/she doesn't want to do or to things that may get him/her into trouble?	1	2	3	4	5

Comments:

39. Does your child accept being told no without becoming upset?	1	2	3	4	5

Comments:

40. Does your child choose acceptable activities on his/her own when feeling bored?	1	2	3	4	5

Comments:

FIGURE 3   Child Skill Checklist

Directions: Ask children to point to the picture on the Child Skill Response Record corresponding to each question (rabbit, teddy bear, cat, etc.), listen carefully as you read the question, then color the face that shows how they feel. Repeat each question at least once.

SESSION 1

1. **Skill 1/rabbit:** Is it easy for you to listen and understand when someone is talking to you?

2. **Skill 2/teddy bear:** Is it easy for you to talk to others in a friendly way?

3. **Skill 3/cat:** Do you tell a person to stop when that person is bothering you without getting upset or mad?

4. **Skill 4/owl:** Do you say thank you or show thanks when someone has said or done something nice for you?

5. **Skill 5/elephant:** Do you tell about things that you do a good job with?

6. **Skill 6/flower:** Is it easy for you to ask in a friendly way when you need help?

7. **Skill 7/pig:** Is it easy for you to ask a favor of someone else?

8. **Skill 8/mouse:** Do you ignore others when they are acting silly?

9. **Skill 9/dog:** Do you ask questions about things you don't understand?

10. **Skill 10/bird:** Do you know what to do when directions are given?

FIGURE 3   Child Skill Checklist (cont'd)

SESSION 2

1. **Skill 11/rabbit:** Do you keep trying when something is hard to do?

2. **Skill 12/teddy bear:** When you want or need something from a teacher or parent who is busy, do you interrupt in a nice way?

3. **Skill 13/cat:** When you walk by somebody you know a little bit, do you smile and say hi?

4. **Skill 14/owl:** Can you tell when someone is sad or mad by how they look?

5. **Skill 15/elephant:** Is it easy for you to join in a game if you want to play?

6. **Skill 16/flower:** Is it easy for you to wait your turn when playing a game?

7. **Skill 17/pig:** Is it easy for you to share toys with friends?

8. **Skill 18/mouse:** Do you notice when someone needs or wants help and try to help them?

9. **Skill 19/dog:** Is it easy for you to ask a friend to play?

10. **Skill 20/bird:** When playing a game, do you play fair?

SESSION 3

1. **Skill 21/rabbit:** Is it easy for you to say how you feel (mad, happy, frustrated)?

2. **Skill 22/teddy bear:** Do you still feel OK if you are left out of a game or activity?

3. **Skill 23/cat:** When you feel upset, is it easy for you to talk about why you're upset?

4. **Skill 24/owl:** When you feel afraid, do you talk to somebody about it?

5. **Skill 25/elephant:** Can you tell if somebody else is feeling mad, sad, or afraid by what the person says?

6. **Skill 26/flower:** Is it easy for you to show the people you like that you like them?

7. **Skill 27/pig:** When somebody teases you, can you keep from being upset?

8. **Skill 28/mouse:** Is it easy for you to stay in control when you are mad?

9. **Skill 29/dog:** Can you tell what is fair or not fair?

10. **Skill 30/bird:** If a problem happens, can you think of different ways to handle it—ways that won't get you into trouble?

SESSION 4

1. **Skill 31/rabbit:** Do you accept your punishment when you've done something wrong without getting mad or upset?

2. **Skill 32/teddy bear:** When you feel tense or upset, is it easy for you to calm down?

3. **Skill 33/cat:** When you make a mistake on an activity or in a game, do you still feel OK?

4. **Skill 34/owl:** Do you tell the truth if you have done something wrong?

5. **Skill 35/elephant:** Can you keep from telling on someone else who does something wrong?

FIGURE 3 Child Skill Checklist (cont'd)

6. **Skill 36/flower:** If you lose at a game, can you keep from becoming upset or angry?

7. **Skill 37/pig:** Do you still feel OK if you are not first at a game or activity?

8. **Skill 38/mouse:** Is it easy to say no to something a friend wants you to do that you don't want to do or that might get you into trouble?

9. **Skill 39/dog:** When you are told no to something you want to do, can you keep from becoming upset?

10. **Skill 40/bird:** When you feel bored, can you choose something to do?

FIGURE 4   Child Skill Response Record

Name _____ Birth Date _____

School/Program _____

Teacher/Evaluator _____ Assessment Date _____

1.

2.

3.

4.

5.

6.

7.

8.

9.

10.

FIGURE 5   Skill Situations Measure

Directions: Read each situation below and ask the child to respond either verbally or by demonstrating a solution. Record the child's responses on the Skill Situations Response Record.

1. **Listening:** Opie starts telling Lila about the things he did over the weekend. What should Lila do?

2. **Using Nice Talk:** If Lila needed to ask to borrow somebody's crayons, how should she ask?

3. **Using Brave Talk:** Opie was playing with a toy car and a friend took it from him. What should Opie say or do?

4. **Saying Thank You:** Opie's friend gave him a box of crayons because he couldn't find his. What should Opie say or do?

5. **Rewarding Yourself:** If Opie made a really neat picture with the crayons, what could he say about the job he did?

6. **Asking for Help:** If Lila was making a picture but was having trouble, what should she do?

7. **Asking a Favor:** The whole class is watching a movie. Everyone is sitting in chairs, and it's crowded. Lila can't see from where she is sitting. What should Lila say or do?

8. **Ignoring:** Lila is supposed to be doing her work, but some friends across the room are acting silly. What should Lila do?

9. **Asking a Question:** In school the teacher tells the class how to do an activity, but Lila doesn't understand. What should she do?

10. **Following Directions:** In school, the teacher is giving directions to the class. She is telling them to put their work in their cubbies and sit on the carpet for a story. What should Opie do?

11. **Trying When It's Hard:** The teacher gives Lila an activity to do that's just a little bit hard for her. What should Lila do when she gets this activity?

12. **Interrupting:** Lila needs the scissors to cut out a picture, and she doesn't know where they are. The teacher is busy with another child. What should Lila do?

13. **Greeting Others:** Opie was in the hall and walked by somebody he knew a little bit. What should Opie do to show that he is friendly?

14. **Reading Others:** Lila sees Opie walking with his head down and a frown on his face. How do you think Opie feels?

15. **Joining In:** Lila sees a group of kids playing a game and decides that she'd like to play, too. What should Lila do?

16. **Waiting Your Turn:** Lila and Opie are playing a game, but they will need to take turns. What should Opie do while Lila is taking her turn?

17. **Sharing:** Opie is playing with the toy dishes in the play kitchen. Lila wants to play with them, too. How could they both play with the dishes?

18. **Offering Help:** Opie notices that a friend has a lot to carry and that he's having trouble opening the door to the classroom. What should Opie do?

19. **Asking Someone to Play:** Lila is playing a game by herself. She thinks that it would be more fun to have a friend play, too. Lila looks around and sees somebody sitting by herself. What should Lila do?

20. **Playing a Game:** Opie is playing Candy Land with some friends. He really wants to win. Opie thinks that next time it's his turn, he might move more spaces than he is supposed to. What should Opie do?

FIGURE 5 Skill Situations Measure (cont'd)

21. **Knowing Your Feelings:** Lila is not feeling very good. Her body inside is tight and she feels like she wants to cry. How do you think Lila feels?

22. **Feeling Left Out:** Lila and Opie are good friends. But during free play, Lila is playing with a different friend, and she isn't asking Opie to play, too. Opie feels left out. What should he do?

23. **Asking to Talk:** Opie acts as if he is really upset about something. What should Opie do?

24. **Dealing with Fear:** In school, Lila's mom usually comes to get her right after snack time and nap. But today, she hasn't come yet. Lila keeps watching for her mom, but she is very afraid. What should Lila do about feeling this way?

25. **Deciding How Someone Feels:** Lila's best friend told her that she wouldn't play with her. How do you think Lila feels?

26. **Showing Affection:** Lila sees a friend she really likes a lot. How should Lila show that she likes this friend?

27. **Dealing with Teasing:** Opie is outside on the playground and a child starts teasing him. He's calling Opie names that are not nice. What should Opie do?

28. **Dealing with Feeling Mad:** Lila is very mad. What things should Lila do so she won't feel so mad?

29. **Deciding If It's Fair:** Lila was coloring with the school's markers. She had six different colors of markers. Opie wanted to color, too, but Lila told him to get his own markers. Was this fair?

30. **Solving a Problem:** Opie has a problem. He forgot to bring his lunch to school. What could Opie do?

31. **Accepting Consequences:** Lila hit a friend because she was mad. The teacher told her to sit in the time-out chair. What should she do while she is in time-out?

32. **Relaxing:** Opie was upset at school, and his teacher told him to relax. What should Opie do to relax?

33. **Dealing with Mistakes:** Opie made a mistake on his activity— he was supposed to color the picture instead of cutting it out. What should Opie do?

34. **Being Honest:** Lila was angry and hit a friend. The teacher asked Lila if she hit her friend. What could Lila say?

35. **Knowing When to Tell:** Opie sees another child do something he isn't supposed to do. The child got out the markers before it was time. What should Opie do?

36. **Dealing with Losing:** Lila played a game with a friend. Lila lost the game. What should Lila say or do?

37. **Wanting to Be First:** Opie likes to ride in the toy car at school. The teacher told another child that she could play with the car first; Opie could play with it next. What should Opie do?

38. **Saying No:** Lila's friend wants her to cross the street without an adult with her. Lila knows she'll get into trouble if she does this. What should Lila do or say?

39. **Accepting No:** Opie wants to go to a friend's house to play. Opie's mother says that it's too close to dinner time and he can't go. What should Opie do?

40. **Deciding What to Do:** Lila is bored—all of her friends are gone for the day and there is no one to play with. What should Lila do?

FIGURE 6 Skill Situations Response Record

Name _____ Birth Date _____

School/Program _____

Teacher/Evaluator _____

Assessment Date _____

1. Listening

☐ Prosocial response   ☐ Aggressive response   ☐ Withdrawn response   ☐ No response or I don't know

Comments:

2. Using Nice Talk

☐ Prosocial response   ☐ Aggressive response   ☐ Withdrawn response   ☐ No response or I don't know

Comments:

3. Using Brave Talk

☐ Prosocial response   ☐ Aggressive response   ☐ Withdrawn response   ☐ No response or I don't know

Comments:

4. Saying Thank You

☐ Prosocial response ☐ Aggressive response ☐ Withdrawn response ☐ No response or I don't know

Comments:

5. Rewarding Yourself

☐ Prosocial response ☐ Aggressive response ☐ Withdrawn response ☐ No response or I don't know

Comments:

6. Asking for Help

☐ Prosocial response ☐ Aggressive response ☐ Withdrawn response ☐ No response or I don't know

Comments:

7. Asking a Favor

☐ Prosocial response ☐ Aggressive response ☐ Withdrawn response ☐ No response or I don't know

Comments:

8. Ignoring

☐ Prosocial response ☐ Aggressive response ☐ Withdrawn response ☐ No response or I don't know

Comments:

FIGURE 6 Skill Situations Response Record (cont'd)

9. Asking a Question

☐ Prosocial response ☐ Aggressive response ☐ Withdrawn response ☐ No response or I don't know

Comments:

10. Following Directions

☐ Prosocial response ☐ Aggressive response ☐ Withdrawn response ☐ No response or I don't know

Comments:

11. Trying When It's Hard

☐ Prosocial response ☐ Aggressive response ☐ Withdrawn response ☐ No response or I don't know

Comments:

12. Interrupting

☐ Prosocial response ☐ Aggressive response ☐ Withdrawn response ☐ No response or I don't know

Comments:

13. Greeting Others

☐ Prosocial response ☐ Aggressive response ☐ Withdrawn response ☐ No response or I don't know

Comments:

14. Reading Others

☐ Prosocial response ☐ Aggressive response ☐ Withdrawn response ☐ No response or I don't know

Comments:

15. Joining In

☐ Prosocial response ☐ Aggressive response ☐ Withdrawn response ☐ No response or I don't know

Comments:

16. Waiting Your Turn

☐ Prosocial response ☐ Aggressive response ☐ Withdrawn response ☐ No response or I don't know

Comments:

17. Sharing

☐ Prosocial response ☐ Aggressive response ☐ Withdrawn response ☐ No response or I don't know

Comments:

18. Offering Help

☐ Prosocial response ☐ Aggressive response ☐ Withdrawn response ☐ No response or I don't know

Comments:

FIGURE 6   Skill Situations Response Record (cont'd)

19. Asking Someone to Play

☐ Prosocial response ☐ Aggressive response ☐ Withdrawn response ☐ No response or I don't know

Comments:

20. Playing a Game

☐ Prosocial response ☐ Aggressive response ☐ Withdrawn response ☐ No response or I don't know

Comments:

21. Knowing Your Feelings

☐ Prosocial response ☐ Aggressive response ☐ Withdrawn response ☐ No response or I don't know

Comments:

22. Feeling Left Out

☐ Prosocial response ☐ Aggressive response ☐ Withdrawn response ☐ No response or I don't know

Comments:

23. Asking to Talk

☐ Prosocial response ☐ Aggressive response ☐ Withdrawn response ☐ No response or I don't know

Comments:

24. Dealing with Fear

☐ Prosocial response   ☐ Aggressive response   ☐ Withdrawn response   ☐ No response or I don't know

Comments:

25. Deciding How Someone Feels

☐ Prosocial response   ☐ Aggressive response   ☐ Withdrawn response   ☐ No response or I don't know

Comments:

26. Showing Affection

☐ Prosocial response   ☐ Aggressive response   ☐ Withdrawn response   ☐ No response or I don't know

Comments:

27. Dealing with Teasing

☐ Prosocial response   ☐ Aggressive response   ☐ Withdrawn response   ☐ No response or I don't know

Comments:

28. Dealing with Feeling Mad

☐ Prosocial response   ☐ Aggressive response   ☐ Withdrawn response   ☐ No response or I don't know

Comments:

FIGURE 6   Skill Situations Response Record (cont'd)

29. Deciding If It's Fair

☐ Prosocial response   ☐ Aggressive response   ☐ Withdrawn response   ☐ No response or I don't know

Comments:

30. Solving a Problem

☐ Prosocial response   ☐ Aggressive response   ☐ Withdrawn response   ☐ No response or I don't know

Comments:

31. Accepting Consequences

☐ Prosocial response   ☐ Aggressive response   ☐ Withdrawn response   ☐ No response or I don't know

Comments:

32. Relaxing

☐ Prosocial response   ☐ Aggressive response   ☐ Withdrawn response   ☐ No response or I don't know

Comments:

33. Dealing with Mistakes

☐ Prosocial response   ☐ Aggressive response   ☐ Withdrawn response   ☐ No response or I don't know

Comments:

34. Being Honest

☐ Prosocial response ☐ Aggressive response ☐ Withdrawn response ☐ No response or I don't know

Comments:

35. Knowing When to Tell

☐ Prosocial response ☐ Aggressive response ☐ Withdrawn response ☐ No response or I don't know

Comments:

36. Dealing with Losing

☐ Prosocial response ☐ Aggressive response ☐ Withdrawn response ☐ No response or I don't know

Comments:

37. Wanting to Be First

☐ Prosocial response ☐ Aggressive response ☐ Withdrawn response ☐ No response or I don't know

Comments:

38. Saying No

☐ Prosocial response ☐ Aggressive response ☐ Withdrawn response ☐ No response or I don't know

Comments:

FIGURE 6   Skill Situations Response Record (cont'd)

39. Accepting No

☐ Prosocial response   ☐ Aggressive response   ☐ Withdrawn response   ☐ No response or I don't know

Comments:

40. Deciding What to Do

☐ Prosocial response   ☐ Aggressive response   ☐ Withdrawn response   ☐ No response or I don't know

Comments:

FIGURE 7   Skills Grouping Chart

	Names									
I: Beginning Social Skills										
1. Listening										
2. Using Nice Talk										
3. Using Brave Talk										
4. Saying Thank You										
5. Rewarding Yourself										
6. Asking for Help										
7. Asking a Favor										
8. Ignoring										
II: School-Related Skills										
9. Asking a Question										
10. Following Directions										
11. Trying When It's Hard										
12. Interrupting										
III: Friendship-Making Skills										
13. Greeting Others										
14. Reading Others										
15. Joining In										
16. Waiting Your Turn										
17. Sharing										
18. Offering Help										
19. Asking Someone to Play										
20. Playing a Game										

FIGURE 7 Skills Grouping Chart (cont'd)

	Names									
IV: Dealing with Feelings										
21. Knowing Your Feelings										
22. Feeling Left Out										
23. Asking to Talk										
24. Dealing with Fear										
25. Deciding How Someone Feels										
26. Showing Affection										
V: Alternatives to Aggression										
27. Dealing with Teasing										
28. Dealing with Feeling Mad										
29. Deciding If It's Fair										
30. Solving a Problem										
31. Accepting Consequences										
VI: Dealing with Stress										
32. Relaxing										
33. Dealing with Mistakes										
34. Being Honest										
35. Knowing When to Tell										
36. Dealing with Losing										
37. Wanting to Be First										
38. Saying No										
39. Accepting No										
40. Deciding What to Do										

FIGURE 8 Progress Summary Sheet

Name _____

Date _____

	Teacher pretest score Date:	Child pretest score Date:	Teacher posttest score Date:	Child posttest score Date:	Performance change Pretest-posttest Teacher	Child
I: Beginning Social Skills						
1. Listening						
2. Using Nice Talk						
3. Using Brave Talk						
4. Saying Thank You						
5. Rewarding Yourself						
6. Asking for Help						
7. Asking a Favor						
8. Ignoring						
II: School-Related Skills						
9. Asking a Question						
10. Following Directions						
11. Trying When It's Hard						
12. Interrupting						
III: Friendship-Making Skills						
13. Greeting Others						
14. Reading Others						
15. Joining In						
16. Waiting Your Turn						
17. Sharing						
18. Offering Help						
19. Asking Someone to Play						
20. Playing a Game						

61

FIGURE 8 Progress Summary Sheet (cont'd)

	Teacher pretest score / Date:	Child pretest score / Date:	Teacher posttest score / Date:	Child posttest score / Date:	Performance change / Pretest-posttest Teacher	Child
IV: Dealing with Feelings						
21. Knowing Your Feelings						
22. Feeling Left Out						
23. Asking to Talk						
24. Dealing with Fear						
25. Deciding How Someone Feels						
26. Showing Affection						
V: Alternatives to Aggression						
27. Dealing with Teasing						
28. Dealing with Feeling Mad						
29. Deciding If It's Fair						
30. Solving a Problem						
31. Accepting Consequences						
VI: Dealing with Stress						
32. Relaxing						
33. Dealing with Mistakes						
34. Being Honest						
35. Knowing When to Tell						
36. Dealing with Losing						
37. Wanting to Be First						
38. Saying No						
39. Accepting No						
40. Deciding What to Do						

FIGURE 9 Sample Teacher Record

Name __Cody R.__

School/Program __Windsor Preschool__   Teacher __Williams__

Objective __Increase positive peer relationships__   Dates of Instruction __9/10/90__ to __9/14/90__

Skill __Sharing (#17)__

Date	Role-play performance — Main actor	Coactor	Feedback participation	Homework (Level assigned/completed)	Transfer training notes
9/10		✓	stated step followed	Level 1	
9/11	✓		offered an idea on how to share	(Level 1)	
9/12		✓		(Level 2)	Needed prompting to share glue during art.
9/13	✓		reminded friend of skill steps	Level 2	
9/14	✓			(Level 2)	During free play, when a child tried to take a toy, said "We can play together."

Note: Circle the level of homework when the child completes it.

63

CHAPTER 4

Planning and Beginning Skillstreaming Instruction

This chapter will describe the procedures necessary to plan and begin Skillstreaming at the preschool and kindergarten levels. We will discuss the instructional setting and materials needed; possible instructional variations; frequency and length of sessions; incorporation of Skillstreaming into the curriculum; the role of parents, administrators, and support staff; selection of group leaders; and group management. Also included are guidelines for teacher preparation and excerpts from a typical introductory Skillstreaming session.

INSTRUCTIONAL SETTING

Whenever possible, the setting for Skillstreaming should be the classroom or another location in which the children spend the majority of their time. Research provides two very important reasons in support of this recommendation. First, because the target child's peers will also have received the same instruction, they will be more likely to assist the skill-deficient child in performing the skill by providing encouragement and feedback as the child practices the newly learned behavior. Second, because generalization from the teaching setting to the application setting does not occur automatically, carrying out training in the setting in which the child will most often need the prosocial skill (i.e., the natural environment of the classroom) will help the learning to generalize.

It is important to note that, whenever possible, instruction should also occur in alternative environments in which the skill is needed, such as the playground, hallway, or school cafeteria. When a prosocial skill is particularly relevant to easily accessible environments, the modeling and role playing should occur in these environments. For the child who has been mainstreamed into a non-special-education group, this means providing instruction in this setting as well as the special education classroom.

Occasionally, it may be necessary to provide skill instruction in another, more artificial environment, such as a counselor's office or a special education resource room. This can and should be done in cases in which the child needs additional help in learning the prosocial skill, but such settings are not recommended either for ongoing instruction or as the only environments for training.

Within the classroom itself, a special space should be set aside for the majority of group instruction. This most often is an area of the classroom where the youngsters can sit cross-legged on the floor in a semicircle, allowing for the modeling display of the skill's behavioral steps, participant role plays, and the creative use of available furniture and supplies. (Some teachers have found it necessary for the children to sit in chairs or on individual carpet samples to create distance between children and thus minimize potential behavior problems.)

If co-leaders are present, one group leader assists youngsters in following the skill steps during individual role plays while the other leader or leaders sit among the children to provide reinforcement for desirable group behavior and to intervene with those who may be in need of additional instruction or behavioral control. Co-leaders may also wish to position themselves near particular children who tend to withdraw from the group or who may become easily excited or restless. Establishing close proximity to such students may prevent behavior problems that might otherwise disrupt the instruction.

MATERIALS

Most of the materials needed to implement Skillstreaming groups already exist in the classroom. If a game or particular toy is an important part of the role play, the actual object should be used whenever possible. If an object is unavailable, classroom materials can be used to simulate it. For example, if a couch is needed to role play a situation occurring in the home, several chairs could be pushed together. Alternatively, toys, games, or other materials can be brought from home.

The use of such props is based upon the important principle of identical elements, discussed in chapter 2. This rule states that the greater the similarities between the teaching and real-life setting (i.e., the greater the number of physical and interpersonal qualities they share), the greater the likelihood that the child will transfer skills from one setting to the other. For this reason, items the children normally have access to should be used in modeling displays and role plays.

Using puppets to depict skill performance may heighten children's interest while creating a sense of distance from real life for those children who are reluctant to role play particularly difficult or sensitive skills. However, the use of puppets should not be viewed as a substitute for actual role playing once the children feel more comfortable with their understanding of the behavioral steps.

The separate Program Forms booklet contains all the assessment measures and recording forms included in this book, as well as Skill Step Handouts and awards to reinforce skill use. (For a sample Skill Step Handout, see Figure 10.) Occasionally, the use of other materials is recommended in the skill lesson plans detailed in chapter 6. These materials are optional and may be used at the teacher's discretion.

FIGURE 10   Sample Skill Step Handout

Listening   SKILL 1

STEPS

1. **Look.**

2. **Stay still.**

3. **Think.**

INSTRUCTIONAL VARIATIONS

In general, previous applications of Skillstreaming have been directed toward children and adolescents selected from the larger classroom group (see Goldstein, Sprafkin, Gershaw, & Klein, 1980; McGinnis, Goldstein, Sprafkin, & Gershaw, 1984). However, for two main reasons, it is best that all of the children in a given preschool or kindergarten class be involved in Skillstreaming instruction. First, providing instruction to the whole group may prevent children from developing maladaptive patterns of behavior that may over time become more well established and thus more difficult to change. In other words, the teacher may choose to provide the children with skill strategies and prosocial behaviors on a preventive basis in order to enable them to handle future skill-relevant difficulties. Second, providing instruction to the entire class involves the use of socially competent peers as models for those youngsters with skill deficits or weaknesses. If handled with sensitivity, including skilled peers gives the skill-deficient child a unique advantage. Because the effectiveness of modeling is enhanced when the model is similar to the observer in age and other characteristics, a child who is adept in a skill may be a more effective model than the classroom teacher. In addition, children who are more competent in skill performance can function effectively as coactors in the role-play activities.

Instruction to the entire class can take place in either large or small groups, depending on the number of children and the availability of staff. We recommend a co-leadership model involving co-teachers, teacher associates, and/or other support personnel whenever possible.

Large Groups

General instruction in Skillstreaming and modeling displays can successfully be conducted in view of a group of 20 or more children. Role plays, however, are better carried out in two or more smaller groups. With fewer children in a role-play group, there will be more opportunity for each child to assume the role of the main actor (the person who practices the skill's behavioral steps) and to receive constructive suggestions, encouragement, and reinforcement regarding this effort. The more practice a child has with a particular prosocial skill, the more likely she will be to apply that skill over time and in other environments. Thus, the total group would first meet to generate skill-relevant situations, present the skill steps, and discuss the skill and its modeling. The role plays, feedback, and assigning and reporting of homework would then be done in smaller groups.

Preschool, day care, or special education teachers may likely work with co-teachers or teacher's aides, but kindergarten teachers may not have such help and may be faced with instructing the large group in all aspects of Skillstreaming. Although this approach may be more difficult, large group instruction remains an effective option. In these circumstances, it is particularly important that the teacher gain the attention and involvement of as many children as possible. This can be done by instituting the following practices:

1. Assign group helper roles, such as pointing out the skill steps on a teacher-made chart as they are being role played or choosing different children for each role play.

2. Encourage each child who is not an active participant in the role play to watch for the enactment of a specific skill step, giving each a Skill Step Handout as an aid in remembering the step to watch for.

3. If a particular child's attention seems to wander easily, position that child closest to the ongoing activity of the role play.

4. Walk around the observers as much as possible while still maintaining verbal involvement in the role play.

5. Include more than one child as a coactor in each role play when it is appropriate to do so.

Small Groups

When circumstances allow, young children should be assigned to smaller groups according to common skill needs. At times this may mean that the participating youngsters will not be from the same classroom or even the same age group. Since role playing is more effective when the teaching setting resembles as closely as possible the real-life setting, it is useful to include children whose social environments (e.g., peer group, family) are similar. Selecting the participants from a common peer group will not only make the role-play setting more realistic, but will enhance the likelihood that the child will attempt the skill with similar peers in the natural settings of the classroom or neighborhood.

Situations exist where grouping based strictly on shared skill deficiencies may not be possible. When this is the case, groups may appropriately be formed according to naturally occurring units, such as special education classrooms or residential cottages. When the groups are organized in this manner, it will be necessary for the teacher to target those skills in which the majority of children show a deficit.

The ideal small group size is 8 to 10 children and two teachers (or one teacher and a teacher's aide, parent volunteer, counselor, or other support person). It is often the case that the training will take place with only one teacher, and Skillstreaming has been operated on this basis quite successfully. However, when two leaders are available, they may alternate roles in either guiding the group role plays or attending to the children observing the actions of the role players. As in the large group, each observer is assigned a behavioral step to watch for as the role play progresses. Toward this end, each may be given a Skill Step Handout to help focus attention on that specific step.

Individual Instruction

Although Skillstreaming is primarily designed to be carried out in a group setting, in special cases modifications of this approach can be made to include one-to-one instruction. The child needing additional help in learning a specific skill, the child withdrawing from group involvement, or the child in special education lacking the prerequisites to function as part of the group are examples of those who would benefit from individual instruction. When carried out in this manner, the Skillstreaming components remain the same, but the adult—or a child's peer if this is feasible—serves as the coactor in each role play, providing the feedback except for that elicited from the child himself. It should be noted that a main objective of individual instruction is to include the youngster in the Skillstreaming group as soon as it is reasonable to do so.

FREQUENCY AND LENGTH OF SESSIONS

At the preschool level, skills training sessions should be held on a daily basis, with kindergartners receiving such instruction for a minimum of three sessions per week. Approximately 15 minutes for preschoolers and 15 to 20 minutes for kindergartners should be planned for each session. Both the number and length of the sessions can be increased or reduced depending upon the attention span, interest, and maturity level of the youngsters. Some teachers have found it most beneficial to conduct a 15-minute session early in the day and another 10-minute session later on. Holding the Skillstreaming session early in the day will give the children more opportunity to practice the newly learned behaviors throughout the remainder of the day. Additional time can be planned for supplementary activities related to skill performance, such as those suggested in chapter 6.

INCORPORATION OF SKILLSTREAMING INTO THE CURRICULUM

Recently, some preschools have designated social skills or social development as a distinct curricular area to encourage direct instruction in prosocial skill behaviors. However, though such a distinction may be ideal, it is not necessary that a social skills class be a formal instructional area. Instead, skills training can easily be integrated into subject areas such as health (e.g., dealing with stress, positive peer interaction), safety (e.g., assertiveness, reducing impulsiveness), social studies (e.g., school, family, and community relationships), language arts (e.g., communication and problem-solving skills), and physical education (e.g., cooperation). The teacher who includes Skillstreaming as a major part of instruction should therefore not be concerned that the content areas will be neglected.

ROLE OF OTHER INDIVIDUALS

Parents

Parent involvement can and should be an integral part of the Skillstreaming program. Initially, parents will need to be informed of the teacher's intent to involve the child in this training, for in the past, preschool and kindergarten programs have included such instruction on an incidental teaching basis only. Because many role plays and homework assignments will depict problems that occur at home, children are likely to discuss with parents the ways they are learning to handle such problems in school. Unless parents understand the purpose of the program, they may question why the school is involved with issues that are, at least in part, home-related concerns. Potential misunderstandings can be averted if the parents are kept informed.

The teacher can encourage parent involvement in several ways:

1. Hold an orientation meeting for parents to describe Skillstreaming objectives and ways parents might assist their child in using these skills at home.

2. For parents who are unable to attend this orientation meeting, send home a letter explaining the skills-enhancement goals of the instruction and the activities in which their child will be participating (i.e., observing modeling displays, role playing, giving and receiving feedback, and doing homework assignments).

3. Involve parents in the assessment of their child's skill strengths and weaknesses by requesting that they complete the Parent Skill Checklist (chap. 3, Figure 2) and by talking with them about skills they value in the home environment.

4. Videotape the youngster in a role play and share this videotape with the parents during parent-teacher conferences to encourage further understanding.

5. Frequently inform parents of the child's progress in given skill areas.

6. Invite parents to observe a Skillstreaming group in progress.

7. Teach parents how to use material and social reinforcers, especially praise, to encourage the child's skill use at home.

8. Involve the parents as participants in a Skillstreaming group led by the teacher along with an administrator or school support person.

It is quite likely that the parents are experiencing concerns about the child's social development that are similar to those the teacher has noted in the school setting. Approaching skills training as a cooperative effort between parents and teachers will not only enhance home-school relations, but will provide additional consistency, encouragement, and reinforcement for the child attempting to learn new behaviors.

Administrators

Support from school administrators is highly valued by a teacher beginning any new teaching strategy. Administrators' attitudes toward the value of the strategy – in this case the teaching of prosocial skills – can contribute greatly to the success of the teacher's efforts. Administrators can lend their active support in several ways:

1. Publicly state a belief in the importance of prosocial skills training and verbally encourage the teachers who are implementing this training.

2. Provide positive reinforcement to participating teachers by letting them know of changes noticed in the children's behavior.

3. Become familiar with Skillstreaming and observe the classroom when the group is in session.

4. Offer direct assistance as a group leader, model, or coactor in role plays.

5. Verbally support parent involvement and actively participate in parent orientation meetings and/or parent training sessions.

6. Reinforce children for prosocial skill performance, and, if a child is sent to the office for disciplinary reasons, discuss alternative prosocial skill choices.

7. Publish a notice in the teachers' bulletin and/or school newsletter of the specific skills currently being emphasized so other teachers and parents may reward skill use.

Support Staff

School support staff such as school psychologists, counselors, social workers, and special education consultants can provide valuable assistance to the teacher in planning and carrying out Skillstreaming. A support person may act in the role of co-leader within the classroom setting. Assessment of skill needs, planning of individual group sessions, direct instruction, and evaluation of skill performance can also be done in a team fashion. Other support staff may be very helpful in performing modeling displays and role plays. As noted in chapter 2, increasing the variety of people with whom children can try out their skills enhances the likelihood that the children will generalize their newly learned behavior. The more people who can participate directly with the children, the more the goal of stimulus variability will be achieved.

SELECTION OF GROUP LEADERS

The process involved in Skillstreaming—modeling, role play, performance feedback, and transfer training—is the same sequence used when teaching a child self-help skills (e.g., tying shoelaces) or academic behaviors (e.g., beginning reading). The classroom teacher, therefore, already possesses the necessary background to carry out Skillstreaming. As noted earlier, other school personnel, such as support staff and administrators, can assist the teacher in instruction. Teacher aides or parent volunteers, when trained in Skillstreaming, may also serve as co-leaders.

Regardless of their orientation or background, individuals conducting Skillstreaming groups should have two sets of skills. The first set includes general teaching and group leadership skills, such as enthusiasm, sensitivity, and good communication. The second set consists of skills related specifically to Skillstreaming. These include the following:

1. Knowledge of Skillstreaming (background, goals, and procedures)

2. Ability to orient participating children, support staff members, and parents to Skillstreaming

3. Ability to plan and present live modeling displays

4. Ability to initiate and sustain role playing

5. Ability to present material in a concrete manner

6. Ability to make the skills relevant to the needs of participating children

7. Accuracy and sensitivity in providing encouragement and corrective feedback

8. Ability to deal effectively with group management problems

MANAGING THE GROUP

The variety of activities included in Skillstreaming will keep the enthusiastic attention of most preschoolers and kindergartners within the recommended time frame. It is helpful, however, to offer the children a special sticker (to be put on their clothing or on a classroom chart) or other small reward on completion of each session for behaviors such as group participation, listening, providing feedback, and following classroom rules. If classroom rules have not been previously identified, they should be decided upon, discussed daily with the children to ensure understanding, and posted in the classroom prior to initiating the Skillstreaming session. Rewarding such behaviors with small, material rewards, in addition to praising children's efforts, will help to create positive feelings about learning new prosocial behaviors.

Should behavioral concerns surface in the group, a total group management plan could be tried. This type of plan might consist of dropping peanuts in a small jar when the group as a whole or specific youngsters show the desired behaviors, then allowing everyone to eat the peanuts when the jar is full. Other plans could include dropping tokens or pennies in the jar and having a special activity, film, or extra recess when the jar is full. Such plans may motivate the group to work cooperatively and may also increase the children's individual motivation. Youngsters who have handicaps relating specifically to behavioral deficits, as well as other children who frequently exhibit behavior problems, may need an even more structured plan to reinforce desirable group behaviors. Suggestions for such plans are provided in chapter 7.

Introductory Skillstreaming Session

With children of preschool and kindergarten age, the primary purpose of the introductory session is to acquaint them with the concept of social skills, illustrate the activities that will be performed, and emphasize that, in this group, they will learn the things they want and need to learn. The following outline suggests a typical format for this session.

A. Introductions

  1. Introduce yourself or others if you or they are not known by the children.

  2. Ask the children to say their names if you or others do not know the children or if the participants are not all from the same classroom.

B. Explanation of prosocial skills and group purpose

   Teacher: First of all, I'm going to tell you what we'll be learning the first thing in the morning every day. We're going to learn the things that you need and want to learn. How many of you like to play games? [Children respond with "Me," "I do," or raised hands.]

Teacher: Well, we're going to learn how to take turns so everybody has more fun in games. Taking turns is a *social skill.* Now, who likes to get in trouble? [Children respond with "Not me," shaking their heads no.] No, getting in trouble isn't much fun, is it? So we'll also learn ways to stay out of trouble, like what to do when you're mad or upset. And we'll all learn to be better friends with each other. These are all kinds of social skills. Do you think you'd like to learn these skills? [Children respond in the affirmative.]

C. Overview of Skillstreaming

1. Describe the four basic Skillstreaming procedures.

Teacher: First, we'll show you how to do a skill. *(modeling)*
Then you'll get to try it. *(role playing)*
And we'll talk about how well you did. *(performance feedback)*
Then you'll get to practice it. *(transfer training)*

2. Demonstrate for the group an example of learning another type of skill (i.e., self-help or academic skill).

Teacher: Let's say I want to learn how to tie my shoes. How am I going to learn to tie my shoes? [Children respond with "Oh, you know"; "Can't you tie your shoes?"; etc.]

Teacher: (holding up a large tennis shoe) I need to learn how to tie my shoe. How will I learn this?

Jordan: Here, I'll show you.

Teacher: Terrific, Jordan. I'm going to need someone to show me how. I'm going to need to watch someone else. That's the first part of learning a skill. What should I do next?

Lisa: You do it . . .

Teacher: You're absolutely right! I'm going to try it. Now, what if it's hard for me—what if I need some help?

Sammy: Jordan will tie it for you.

Teacher: OK. I'd certainly get my shoe tied, but would I learn how to tie it myself? [The group responds "No."]

Teacher: So what I need, then, is someone to tell me what I'm doing that's right and where I've messed up. Would that help me learn? ["Yes," and "Yeah" can be heard from the group.]

Teacher: Then, once I've had someone tell me how to do it better, I'll need lots of practice, right? This is the same way we'll learn social skills.

D. Explanation of the reinforcement system if one will be used and review of classroom rules

Teacher: (pulling a package from a bag) Here I have lots of dinosaur stickers. Who likes dinosaurs? I do! Well, for everyone who follows our classroom rules during social skills class and tries to learn the skills we're working on, I'll have a sticker for you to wear on your shirt at the end of the group.

E. Conclusion

Teacher: We'll have fun learning these new social skills, and we'll help each other learn them. We may also have some special visitors come to the class—we'll have to wait and see! (The teacher then has the children quiet down while she gives the directions for the next activity.)

SUMMARY

This chapter has discussed the steps necessary to plan and organize effective Skillstreaming groups. Table 2 lists the steps that must be accomplished prior to implementing Skillstreaming with young children. Carefully following these steps will foster a reinforcing environment for both participants and group leaders.

TABLE 2 Teacher Preparation Checklist

☐ 1. An area of the classroom has been prepared for carrying out the group (chairs or carpet samples, space for role plays, etc.).

☐ 2. The time of day the group will meet has been scheduled, and the length of sessions has been estimated.

☐ 3. Necessary materials are in hand (Skill Step Handouts, teacher-made skill charts, puppets, etc.).

☐ 4. The group leaders are prepared with respect to their knowledge of Skillstreaming.

☐ 5. Parents and others (e.g., other teachers, administrators) are informed of the goals and strategies that will be used.

☐ 6. The Skill Checklists (teacher, parent, and child; chap. 3, Figures 1–3) have been completed for each target youngster in the group.

☐ 7. Other assessment procedures determined to be useful (one or more of those described in chap. 3) have been completed.

☐ 8. If necessary, a reinforcement system has been planned and explained to the children.

CHAPTER 5

Implementing Skillstreaming Instruction

The present chapter provides the reader with a specific and detailed plan for implementing Skillstreaming instruction. This plan includes (1) enhancing motivation, (2) identifying situations in which the skill is needed, (3) presenting the behavioral steps for the skill, (4) modeling the skill, (5) guiding the role play, (6) giving performance feedback, (7) transfer training, and (8) maintenance.

ENHANCING MOTIVATION

Most young children are likely to be more motivated to learn the behaviors presented in the Skillstreaming group when they feel they need to learn a particular prosocial skill. For example, if a preschooler often feels that he is the brunt of teasing from peers, the child will be more highly motivated to learn Dealing with Teasing (Skill 27) than another skill not as immediately relevant.[1] Information regarding such relevant skill needs can be made by referring to the children's responses on the Child Skill Checklist (chap. 3, Figure 3) and on the Skill Situations Measure (chap. 3, Figure 5), as well as by discussing with the group the day-to-day problems the children encounter. Such discussions should be relatively brief due to the short attention span of this age group. The following types of questions will help stimulate discussion: "Who finds it hard to wait for a turn while playing a game?" "Is it hard for you to share a toy with someone else?" and "Who feels really mad after making a mistake?" Once a list of needed skills is formulated, one skill is then chosen for instruction.

---

[1] The skills mentioned in this chapter are described fully in chapter 6.

Although it is critical that the skills chosen be those the children want and need to learn, it is also important that children be successful in the early stages. Using the selected skill must be more rewarding to the children than engaging in their previous patterns of behavior. Therefore, if it seems unlikely that the children will initially be able to master a skill associated with a highly emotional situation (e.g., Skill 31: Accepting Consequences), it is better to begin instruction with a skill they will have more success in performing.

In addition, carrying out Skillstreaming instruction early in the school day will allow the teacher to enhance motivation by encouraging skill use in naturally occurring social situations (e.g., free play, snack time, recess) and during structured activities (e.g., story time, preacademic activities) throughout the school day. Furthermore, selecting a skill that the children will have the opportunity to use within the teacher's view will allow the teacher to reward the children for applying the skill.

IDENTIFYING SITUATIONS

Following the selection of the skill, children help to generate specific situations in which the skill could be applied. If Dealing with Losing (Skill 36) is chosen, for example, the teacher might ask such questions as "When is it difficult not to win?" or "When do you most like to win?" If the children do not report a specific situation noted by the teacher to be problematic, they can be asked more leading questions, such as "I noticed problems often happen when some of the children are playing kick soccer at recess. Would this be a time when you could use the skill?" Allowing the children to describe situations in which they experience difficulty will further their understanding of when and where the skill can be applied, as well as provide the situations for later modeling and role-play examples.

PRESENTING THE BEHAVIORAL STEPS

The behavioral steps corresponding to the selected prosocial skill are then presented to the group. These steps are listed and illustrated in chapter 6 and on the Skill Step Handouts provided in the Program Forms booklet (for a sample handout, see chap. 4, Figure 10). It is important that the skill steps and illustrations be presented so all group members may easily view them. The teacher should therefore give each child a Skill Step Handout and construct a large chart for each skill containing this same information. The skill chart can be used during instruction and later posted in the classroom so the children can refer to the behavioral steps whenever a real-life situation suggests skill use.

MODELING

Modeling the prosocial skill, or showing the children what to do, is the next procedure. The behavioral skill steps should be modeled in the correct sequence and in a clear and unambiguous way. Generally, the modeling will consist of live vignettes enacted by the teacher and a co-leader. If a co-leader is unavailable, another adult (e.g., a school support person, teacher's aide, principal, or parent volunteer) may help with this part of Skillstreaming. If this is not possible, a reasonably skillful child may serve as a model, with the teacher taking the main role of acting out the behavioral steps. In all instances, it is especially important to rehearse the vignettes carefully prior to performing them, making sure that all of the skill steps are enacted properly and in the correct sequence. Complete scripts for the modeling displays are usually not necessary; instead, the teacher can outline the roles and likely responses during preclass preparations. Even when puppets are used as models to add variety to the Skillstreaming lessons, these modeling display outlines should incorporate the following guidelines.

Depict Relevant Situations

The teacher should plan the modeling displays to depict situations relevant to the real-life problems of the children in the Skillstreaming group. Appropriate content for these modeling displays may be selected on the basis of information from the various assessment instruments detailed in chapter 3 or from group discussion among children. Chapter 6 also suggests possible modeling displays for each of the skills.

Model at Least Two Examples

At least two examples of the skill should be modeled so that the children are exposed to use of the skill in different situations. For example, it may be important for Joanne to learn how to share the playground equipment at recess, but she also needs to see that she can use the same skill for sharing glue and scissors in a classroom activity or sharing toys during free play or with friends or siblings at home. Because instruction for each skill will most often take place over more than one group session, two or more different modeling displays should be planned for each session.

Assign Observers

In order to help the children attend to the modeling display, direct them to the Skill Step Handout or skill chart. Tell the children to watch and listen closely as the models portray the skill. As noted earlier, selecting individual children to watch for each skill step is a good way of focusing attention on the modeling display.

Use a Coping Model

Modeling is more effective when a coping model, or one that struggles a little to achieve the goal of competent skill performance, is presented (Bandura, 1977). When demonstrating Waiting Your Turn (Skill 16), for instance, the model could show slight impatience (e.g., moving his body slightly and folding his arms while watching others take turns in sequence) to illustrate that it is difficult to wait but that the skill can be mastered. Likewise, skills associated with strong emotions, such as Dealing with Teasing (Skill 27) and Dealing with Feeling Mad (Skill 28), require a model to show anger or frustration in an acceptable way (e.g., clenching teeth and frowning). Depicting such models will enhance the children's ability to identify with the model and will likely give them more courage to try the skill themselves.

Use Verbal Mediation

Verbal mediation, or saying aloud what would normally be said to oneself silently, is a valuable and necessary part of both modeling and role playing. Saying the steps aloud as the models or role players are enacting the behaviors demonstrates the cognitive processes underlying skill performance and facilitates learning. For example, in Joining In (Skill 15), the model might say, "I want to ask if I can play, but I'm afraid they might say no. But I'm going to take the chance. OK, the first step is to watch." Likewise, in Knowing When to Tell (Skill 35), the model would recite the skill step in the context of the situation: "Those kids are teasing Jessie. They shouldn't do that. It's a problem, but should I tell? What's the first step?" This type of accompanying narration increases the effectiveness of the modeling display (Bandura, 1977), draws the attention of observers to the specific skill steps, and may also facilitate generalization of the skill (Stokes & Baer, 1977). Verbal mediation also helps to demonstrate a coping model. For example, in Waiting Your Turn Skill 16), the model might say aloud, "It's hard to wait, but I can do it."

Many young children will need to be taught the process of thinking aloud by having them practice while they are engaged in other types of activities (e.g., "Which picture goes with the dog? Look at all of them. Is it the chair? No. Keep looking."). Many activities useful in teaching young children the technique of verbal mediation can be found in the Think Aloud Program, developed by Camp and Bash (1981, 1985).

Depict Positive Outcomes

All modeling displays should depict positive outcomes. In other words, the model's portrayal of the skill should actually work to bring about the desired outcome. For example, if the behavioral steps to Joining In (Skill 15) are shown, then the coactors will accept the model's overture, allowing this person to take part in the ongoing activity. In the initial stages of learning a skill, the children must see that the skill really will work in most situations. Because it has been well-established that the modeling will be more effective when the model is rewarded for the behavior, the model who has used the skill correctly should ideally also receive reinforcement in the form of praise. The teacher may provide this praise, or the model may even praise herself (e.g., "I followed all of the steps. Good for me!").

The following example illustrates some of the main points involved in effective modeling.

EXAMPLE

Teacher: Mr. Williams has an activity to do. He has to cut out an animal shape. But cutting is hard for Mr. Williams, so he's going to use the skill Trying When It's Hard (Skill 11). *(describing the situation)* The steps to this skill are, first, stop and think.

(Co-leader points to this step on the skill chart, then to the next steps in turn.)

Teacher: Then say, "It's hard, but I'll try." The last step is to really try it. *(identifying each step)* Let's watch to see if Mr. Williams follows all of these steps. David, will you watch for the first step? Kara, will you watch for the second? Bobby, the third? *(assignments to the observers)*

Mr. Williams: (sitting at the table with the activity he is to complete, frowning and shaking his head) This is kind of hard. *(thinking aloud/coping model)* So the first thing to do is to stop and

think—getting upset won't help me get this
done. (Mr. Williams looks at the steps on
the skill chart to see the next step.) Now I
need to say, "It's hard, but I'll try." (Mr.
Williams looks determined as he picks up
the scissors.) Now I'm going to really try it!
(Mr. Williams cuts out the animal shape.)
(*positive outcome*) Hey, I did a pretty good
job! (*self-reward*)

Co-leader: (turning to the group) Did Mr. Williams do
all the steps? What about the first step? The
other steps? Good job, Mr. Williams!
(*rewarding the model*)

GUIDING THE ROLE PLAY

Following the modeling display, group discussion should attempt to re-
late the modeled skill to the children's lives outside the Skillstreaming
setting. The teacher should thus elicit comments on the way the steps
portrayed could be applied in situations typically encountered by the
children. These situations form the basis for role playing.

Because role playing in Skillstreaming is intended to serve as behavioral rehearsal or practice for future use of the skill, it is most helpful
to have the group focus on how they might use the skill in a present
and future situation, rather than relating the skill to past events. However, discussions of past events involving skill use can help stimulate
the children to think of times when a similar situation may occur in the
future. In such a case, the hypothetical future situation, rather than the
past event, would be selected for role playing. In any case, the procedures next discussed would be followed.

Select the Actors

If a child has offered a situation in which the skill could be used, that
child is then selected as the main actor to role play the skill's behavioral
steps. More commonly, however, it will be necessary for the teacher to
offer a specific situation, perhaps one generated earlier in group discussion, then ask someone who wants to learn the skill to be the main actor. In cases where no child offers to be the main actor, the teacher will
need to select the participant, asking, for example, "David, will you come
up and help us with this one, please?" The child may wish to choose

a puppet to act as the main actor, with the child serving as the puppeteer.

The main actor then chooses a second child or one of the group leaders to play the role of the other person relevant to the skill problem (e.g., parent, peer, sibling, teacher). It is important that the child choose a coactor who resembles the real-life person in as many ways as possible.

Set the Stage

The teacher then elicits from the main actor any additional information necessary to set the stage for the role play. In order to make the role play as realistic as possible, the teacher should obtain descriptions of the physical setting in which the child is likely to use the skill, the events that precede the problem, and any other relevant information. In the initial stages of Skillstreaming, the teacher will likely need to describe the situation in terms of her own observations of skill need. For example, the teacher might say, "I notice that when we use the markers to draw, there is often a problem using the skill Sharing (Skill 17). Let's do this role play in the art area. Here are the markers and drawing paper."

Conduct the Role Play

The primary purpose of the role play is for the main actor to enact the behavioral steps that have been modeled. Before beginning the role play, the teacher may find it useful to rehearse with the child what to say and do to illustrate each step. The child can then be directed to the Skill Step Handout (see chap. 4, Figure 10) or skill chart and instructed to talk himself through the skill while role playing. Research suggests that such verbal mediation in the role-play setting helps the child restrain impulsiveness and better retain and organize behaviors (Camp & Bash, 1981). At this point, the teacher also needs to remind all of the participants of their responsibilities: The main actor is to follow the behavioral steps; the coactor is to stay in the role of the other person; and the observers are to watch carefully for the performance of the behavioral steps.

During the role play itself, it is the teacher's main responsibility to provide whatever help or coaching the main actor needs in order to keep the role play going according to the behavioral steps. If the role play is clearly going astray, the scene can be stopped, needed instruction can be provided, and the role play can be recommenced with the skill's first behavioral step. The main actor, as well as the group observers, will be assisted in following each of the steps in order if the teacher or co-leader points to each of the behavioral steps on the skill chart as the role play unfolds. It may be necessary to provide the main actor with verbal prompts throughout the role play. In Asking Someone to Play (Skill 19), for example, one such prompt would be "We heard you do the first step; you decided that you wanted to play with someone. Now, you're ready to decide whom you'd like to play with."

Role playing should be continued until all members of the group have had an opportunity to participate as the main actor at least once. This may require more than one session for a given skill. It is important to note that, although the framework (i.e., the behavioral skill steps) of each role play remains the same, the actual content can and should change from role play to role play. It is the problem as it actually occurs, or could occur, in each child's real-life environment that should be the focus of each child's role play. In addition, role playing the skill a number of times with different people and in a variety of hypothetical situations will increase the likelihood that the child will use the skill in places other than the teaching setting (Stokes & Baer, 1977).

One type of situation in which it is preferable for the teacher or co-leader to assume the coactor role is when inappropriate behaviors must be enacted as part of the role-play situation, as required in role playing Dealing with Teasing (Skill 27). Children should not be placed in the position of exhibiting inappropriate behaviors even when the goal is to create a realistic role play. When children play the part of tormentors, they may easily become carried away, losing the main point of the role play. In brief, we do not want children to act in the role-play setting in ways we do not want them to act in real life. It is also beneficial to have a leader participate as the coactor when an adult role needs to be realistically portrayed. Finally, having leaders as coactors or as puppeteers may be particularly helpful when dealing with less verbal or more hesitant role players. The following example illustrates some of the main points involved in guiding the role play.

EXAMPLE

Interrupting   SKILL 12

STEPS

1. **Decide if you need to.**

2. **Walk to the person.**

3. **Wait.**

4. **Say "Excuse me."**

Preparation for Role Play

1. Sara states that she often gets into trouble at home for interrupting her mother when she is talking on the telephone. Sara volunteers to role play the skill, which has just been modeled.

2. Sara chooses the teacher, Ms. Franson, as the person who reminds her most of her mother.

3. Several chairs are pushed together to resemble the couch in Sara's home. A toy telephone is used to represent the real telephone.

4. Sara describes the situation that she needs help getting her bike out of the garage so that she can ride it outside. She states that her mother typically will ignore her, then, as Sara persists, her mother gives her "mad looks." Then when her mother gets off the phone, she scolds Sara.

5. The teacher reviews the skill steps and reminds Sara to look at the skill chart displaying the steps and do her thinking out loud.

6. Remaining group participants are selected to watch for Sara's performance of particular skill steps.

7. The co-leader assists Sara in the role play by pointing to each of the steps on the skill chart and monitors the attention of the remaining group members.

Role Play

(Ms. Franson, playing the role of Sara's mother, is pretending to talk on the telephone. The co-leader points to the first step.)

> Sara: Mom is on the phone. Decide if I need to interrupt. I want my bike. Mom's been talking a long time.

(The co-leader points to the second step.)

> Sara: (walking up as "Mom" continues to talk) I walk to Mom. Excuse me?

> Co-leader: Hold it, Sara. What's the third step?

Sara:	Wait.
Co-leader:	That's right. Wait until your mother gives you some sign that it's OK to talk.
Sara:	OK.
Co-leader:	(pointing to the first step) Let's start again.
Sara:	Mom's on the phone. It's been a long time. I want my bike.

(Co-leader points to the next step.)

Sara:	(walking up to "Mom") I walk to Mom.

(Co-leader points to the third step.)

Sara:	I wait. (Co-leader smiles and nods her head as Sara continues to wait.)
Ms. Franson:	(to the other person on the line) Can you hold on a minute? (She then looks at Sara.)
Sara:	Excuse me. I want my bike. I can't get it by myself.
Ms. Franson:	OK, Sara. I'll be right there to help you. You've waited quite a while. (to the person on the line) I need to say goodbye now.

PERFORMANCE FEEDBACK

A brief performance feedback period follows each role play. Feedback helps the main actor find out how well he followed the behavioral steps, assesses the impact of the role play on the coactor, and provides the main actor with encouragement to try the skill outside the group. In addition, encouraging group members to participate in feedback focuses their attention on the role play and helps prevent boredom and potential behavior problems.

Immediately following the role play, the coactor is first asked about her reactions. "What did you think when he asked to join in?" or "How did you feel when she said no to you?" are examples of the types of questions helpful in eliciting the coactor's feedback.

Next, the children assigned to watch for each specific skill step report on how well the main actor did in following each one. Because Skill-streaming is a behavioral approach, the feedback concerning whether or not a step was performed should focus on overt behaviors. Toward this end, the teacher should ask questions such as "How do you know?" or "What did she do?" to emphasize this behavioral focus and teach observers to provide concrete evidence to back up their feedback. It is important to point out in this regard that several of the skills require the main actor to think or to decide. The only way observers can be sure this step has been followed is for the main actor to think out loud. Observers can then be asked, "How do you know this step was followed?" Their likely response will be "Because he said it" or the like.

After observers have commented on the execution of the skill steps, other group members may comment about skill step performance or other aspects of the role play (e.g., "He was friendly"; "He wasn't mad"). Any discrepancies between the main actor's verbal and nonverbal cues should be brought out at this point (e.g., the main actor has said that she was mad, yet she was smiling). Asking questions like "How do you know he asked in a friendly way?" and eliciting answers such as "He smiled" will also emphasize the importance of nonverbal language.

Next, the teacher and co-leader should comment on how well the behavioral steps were followed and provide social reinforcement (praise, approval, encouragement) for close following. It is generally desirable to have the observers evaluate the main actor's role play before leaders give their responses; however, leaders may need to model appropriate and helpful feedback if the observers are unsure of what type of feedback is expected of them or if their comments are not constructive. Modeled feedback could include suggestions for what the role player could do to be more successful, constructive reminders to include a specific skill step, and comments pertaining to the feelings of the role player or to the consistency of the role player's body language with verbal responses. Once the group's focus is directed toward the main actor's positive behavior and the children feel more confident in giving appropriate comments, leaders can resume eliciting feedback from the group members first.

Finally, after receiving feedback from the coactor, observers, other group members, and leaders, the main actor is invited to comment on the role play.

In all aspects of feedback, it is important that the leaders maintain the behavioral focus of Skillstreaming and that this focus be a positive one. As was required of the observers, leader feedback must be directed to the presence or absence of specific, concrete behaviors and not take the form of general evaluative comments. In addition, a negative comment should always be followed by a constructive one, such as how a particular skill or skill step might be improved. At minimum, a poor performance (a major departure from the behavioral steps) can be praised as "a good try." It is critical that children be successful in their performance. Therefore, children failing to follow the behavioral steps should be given the opportunity to role play these same steps again after receiving corrective feedback, reteaching, or direct guidance.

TRANSFER TRAINING

Several studies indicate that although the combination of modeling, role play, and feedback is a successful strategy for teaching skills, behaviors learned in this manner may not be maintained over time or generalize outside of the teaching setting unless specific techniques are implemented to assist this transfer (Goldstein, 1981). As noted earlier, reinforcement in the form of praise, stickers, or other rewards following participation in role-play and performance feedback can help effect skill transfer and generalization.[2] The techniques described below can also help achieve this goal. It cannot be stressed too strongly that, without attempts such as these to maximize transfer, the entire teaching effort is in jeopardy.

Assign Homework

We have found the use of homework assignments to be particularly successful in enhancing transfer. In these assignments, children who have successfully role played a given skill as main actors are instructed to try in their own real-life settings the behaviors they have practiced during the teaching session. Children should not be expected to perform the skill perfectly when first using it, however. Instead, reinforcement should be given as performance becomes more and more like the ideal. To encourage children to attempt further real-life skill use, it is important that initial experiences with homework assignments be successful.

Two levels of homework are suggested. The first is used until the teacher is reasonably certain that the child has a good understanding of the expected performance of the given skill. The child can then be instructed to practice the skill by completing the second level of homework.

Homework I

In this first level, the child thinks of situations either at home or school in which she would like to or needs to practice the skill. When Skillstreaming is still fairly new to the group, the teacher may need to provide strong guidance in selecting these situations. It is especially

---

[2] For more discussion of the importance of reinforcement, see chapter 7.

helpful if the situations chosen are the same ones the child has role played. On the Homework I Report (see example in Figure 11), the teacher lists the child's name, the date the assignment is made, the name of the skill the child will use, and the appropriate skill steps and illustrations.[3] Together, the teacher and the child decide on the person with whom the child will try the skill and when she will actually make the attempt (e.g., during free play, outside at home after school). These decisions should be illustrated on the Homework Report in picture format by either the child or the teacher. After the child actually tries the skill, she evaluates how well she followed the behavioral steps by coloring in one of the three faces on the form. Because many preschoolers may not be able to make accurate self-evaluations when they first begin this procedure, the teacher should discuss the child's reasons for her choice. In addition, it must be made clear to the child that this evaluation pertains to how well she followed the skill steps rather than how well the skill actually worked.

Homework II

The child who has been successful with Homework I assignments is ready to attempt monitoring his own skill use. With assistance from the child, the teacher completes the relevant information on the Homework II Report (see example in Figure 12), including the behavioral skill steps and illustrations for the target skill. Then, throughout the course of the day, the child colors a happy face whenever he practices the skill steps and draws a picture of when or with whom he used the skill. If the child does not enjoy drawing, it is acceptable if the person with whom he used the skill signs or initials the space provided.

Using homework assignments

The first part of each Skillstreaming session is devoted to presenting and discussing the children's homework assignments, which the teacher has previously reviewed on an individual basis. This individual review is suggested so that a child who may have been unsuccessful can be spared the possible embarrassment of sharing this failure publicly. When children have made an effort to complete their homework assignments, the teacher provides social reinforcement for this achievement. A child who repeatedly fails to complete the homework is likely to need

---

[3] The steps and illustrations for each of the 40 skills are included in the Program Forms booklet and in chapter 6 of this volume. The teacher may attach a copy of these steps and their illustrations to the homework reports as needed. Alternatively, the teacher and child may choose to list and illustrate the skill steps themselves.

FIGURE 11 Sample Homework I Report

Name _____ *Alex* _____ Date _*10/15/90*_

Skill _**Dealing with Teasing (#27)**_

STEPS

1. **Stop and think.**

2. **Say "Please stop."**

3. **Walk away.**

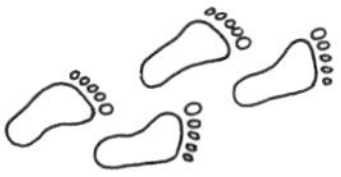

Who?

Susan

When? Recess

How I did

FIGURE 12   Sample Homework II Report

Name _____ Sara _____ Date _10/15/90_

Skill _Dealing with Feeling Mad (#28)_

STEPS

1. **Stop and think.**

2. **Choose.**

   a. Turtle.

   b. Relax.

   c. Ask to talk.

3. **Do it.**

I did it!

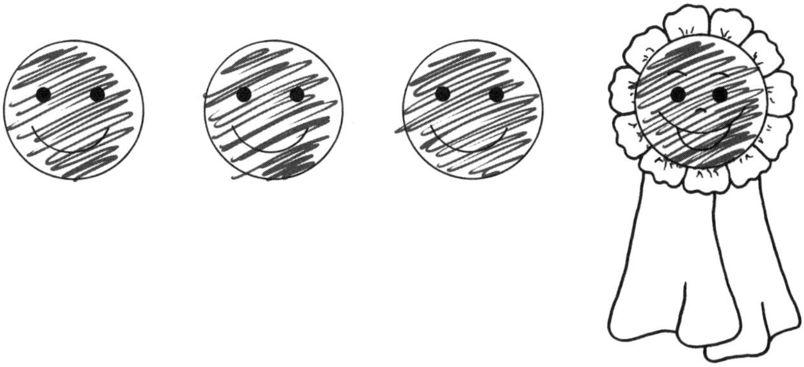

either further skill instruction or more potent reinforcers for homework completion (i.e., tangible rewards).

MAINTENANCE

Maintenance assignments, designed to encourage the child's continued use of previously learned skills, should be used after successful completion of the first two levels of homework. Both individual and group methods may be employed to enhance the effectiveness of the Skillstreaming process. These involve the following techniques.

Self-Monitoring

The child's continued use of a learned skill should be encouraged by ongoing monitoring of skill use. The Sample Self-Monitoring Form (see Figure 13) is associated with one such plan. In using this form, the teacher identifies the skill for practice and the child colors a spot on the giraffe each time the skill is performed. When all the spots have been colored, the child is allowed to keep the giraffe as a reinforcer. A stronger reinforcer (e.g., an additional tangible reward or special privilege) may be provided, particularly if the child has been successful in achieving repeated skill performance to remediate a particularly problematic behavior. This type of plan lends itself best to skills that can be performed in view of the teacher, especially for younger preschoolers, who may not accurately report their own behavior. Examples of other self-monitoring forms are included in the Program Forms booklet or may be created as needed by the teacher.

Group Reward Plan

In this procedure, the teacher or group selects a specific target skill on which to focus. Most often, this skill will be one recently taught in the Skillstreaming group or one that the children need an extra reminder to use throughout the day. Each time any child (or even the teacher) performs the skill, a block is colored on the Group Reward Form (for sample, see Figure 14). When all of the blocks have been colored, the entire group earns a special reward, such as a popcorn party, an extra recess period, or a favorite movie. Other types of group plans similar to this example may be created by the teacher. Using a plan in which all group members work together to achieve a common goal helps to create a cooperative spirit in the classroom and will often result in children's reminding one another to use the skill when a situation suggests its use.

FIGURE 13   Sample Self-Monitoring Form

I reached
my goal!

Name _____ *Dawn* _____
Date _____ *10/15/90* _____
Skill _____ *Asking for Help (#6)* _____

FIGURE 14 Sample Group Reward Form

Together we can!

Skill _____ Listening (#1) _____

Skill Tickets

To encourage the continued use of prosocial skills in the school setting, token reinforcers such as the Skill Ticket shown in Figure 15 may be given throughout the school day when individual children use any prosocial skill. The tickets can be accumulated until a given number are earned, then redeemed for a special activity or reward. If necessary, these tickets may also be given in the Skillstreaming group itself to encourage following group rules, role playing, and completing homework assignments. Such tokens should always be paired with verbal praise. It is also important that each child write his or her name on these tickets and that a special place be provided in which to store them.

Skill Notes

Teachers typically send home notes to parents pertaining to preacademic or behavioral achievements. Skill Notes such as the one illustrated in Figure 16 can be completed and sent home with a child who has demonstrated skill use in the classroom or in another school environment. Again, the purpose of such notes is to provide the child with additional reinforcement for prosocial skill use and to communicate to the child's parents which specific skills are being emphasized at school or day care.

Awards

Children are more likely to continue their attempts to use a prosocial skill if they are rewarded by significant others in their environment. Such awards may be given by the teacher, principal, and/or parents.

The Teacher Award is a type of material reinforcer to be given after children have attained proficiency in some or all of the skills included in one of the six main skill groups.[4] Figure 17 illustrates an award given for achievement in Group IV (Dealing with Feelings). These awards may be displayed in the classroom on a bulletin board reserved for this purpose and then taken home by the child to show to parents.

Whenever a teacher or other person in the school environment observes a child using a prosocial skill, the child may be sent to the principal's or director's office to receive a Principal Award, along with words of praise and encouragement. (For a sample Principal Award, see Figure 18.) Such reinforcement from a person in an authority role may provide a strong reinforcer to the child to continue to use prosocial behaviors.

---

[4] The Teacher Award for Beginning Social Skills, included in the Program Forms booklet, may also be used to reinforce individual skills.

FIGURE 15 Sample Skill Ticket

☆ ☆ ☆ ☆ ☆ ☆ ☆ ☆ ☆
☆ Skill Ticket ☆
☆ ☆
☆ ☆
☆ ____*Oliver*____ ☆
Name
☆ ☆ ☆ ☆ ☆ ☆ ☆ ☆ ☆

FIGURE 16 Sample Skill Note

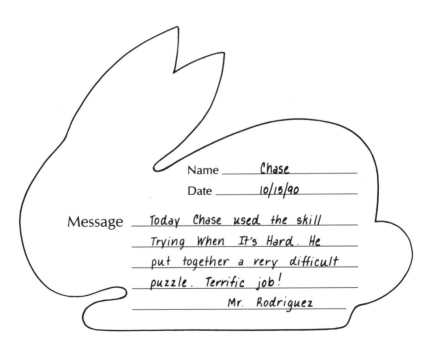

Name _____*Chase*_____
Date _____*10/15/90*_____

Message *Today Chase used the skill*
Trying When It's Hard. He
put together a very difficult
puzzle. Terrific job!
Mr. Rodriguez

FIGURE 17 Sample Teacher Award

Dealing with Feelings Award

Name _____ Ray _____

Date _____ 10/15/90 _____

FIGURE 18 **Sample Principal Award**

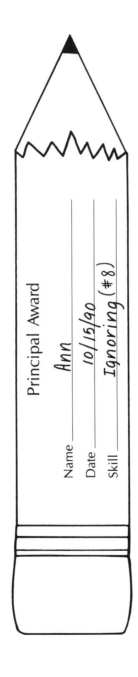

Principal Award

Name _Ann_

Date _10/15/90_

Skill _Ignoring (#8)_

The Parent Award illustrated in Figure 19 is designed to be used by parents who have been involved in a Skillstreaming training session and who will likely notice prosocial skill use in the home setting. The Parent Award lists the prosocial skill parents should watch for, along with instructions to sign the award and return it to school with the child once the skill is observed. The awards can then be displayed in the classroom as appropriate. This method provides additional reinforcement to the child as she attempts skill use outside of the classroom.

Skill Folders

Each child in the Skillstreaming group should keep a Skill Folder to organize materials (e.g., Skill Step Handouts, homework assignments, awards). The child will then have easy access, when needed, to the behavioral steps for skills practiced in the past. To enhance the likelihood that these learned prosocial behaviors will also be used outside of the instructional setting, the teacher may send the child's Skill Folder home on a regular basis. As the child demonstrates prosocial behaviors at home, Parent Awards can be inserted.

SUMMARY

This chapter has described the procedures necessary to begin effective Skillstreaming groups for preschool and kindergarten children. The sequence of Skillstreaming components and step-by-step procedures for conducting sessions have been examined. These steps and the main points associated with them are listed for the reader's convenience in Table 3.

FIGURE 19   Sample Parent Award

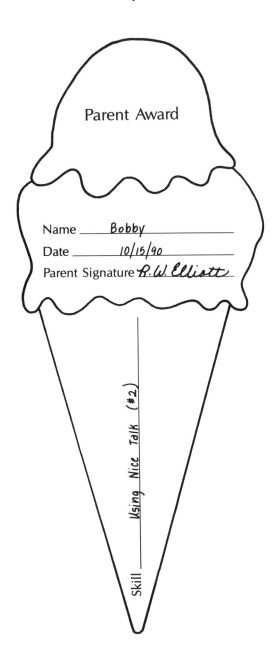

Parent Award

Name _____Bobby_____

Date _____10/15/90_____

Parent Signature _R.W. Elliott_

Skill _____Using Nice Talk (#2)_____

TABLE 3   Outline of Skillstreaming Steps

ENHANCING MOTIVATION

1. Choose skills relevant to the needs of the children as they perceive them.

2. In selecting the initial skills to be taught, choose ones with which the children are likely to be successful.

3. Provide Skillstreaming instruction early to allow children to practice the skills throughout the remainder of the school day.

4. Provide children with reinforcement (e.g., praise, stickers, tokens) when skills are used successfully.

IDENTIFYING SITUATIONS

1. Allow children to identify specific situations in which the skill could be applied.

2. Identify additional skill-relevant situations by observing children's classroom behavior and by questioning participants.

PRESENTING THE BEHAVIORAL STEPS

1. Discuss each skill step and any other relevant information pertaining to each step.

2. Use Skill Step Handouts and a skill chart so the skill steps and illustrations may be easily seen by all group members.

MODELING

1. Use at least two examples for each skill demonstration.

2. Select situations relevant to the children's real-life circumstances.

3. Use modeling displays that demonstrate all the behavioral steps of the skill in the correct sequence.

4. Use modeling displays that depict only one skill at a time. (All extraneous content should be eliminated.)

5. Show the use of a coping model.

TABLE 3 Outline of Skillstreaming Steps (cont'd)

6. Have the model think out loud steps that would ordinarily be thought silently.

7. Depict only positive outcomes.

8. Reinforce the model who has used the skill correctly by using praise, self-reward, etc.

GUIDING THE ROLE PLAY

1. Select as the main actor a child who describes a situation in his own life in which skill use might be helpful.

2. Have the main actor choose a coactor who reminds her most of the person with whom she has the problem.

3. Present relevant information surrounding the real event (i.e., describe the physical setting and events preceding the problem).

4. Use props when appropriate.

5. Review skill steps and direct the main actor to look at the Skill Step Handout or skill chart.

6. Encourage the other group participants to watch for specific skill steps.

7. Instruct the main actor to think out loud.

8. Have one leader assist the main actor (e.g., point to each behavioral step as the role play is carried out); have the other leader, if available, sit among the group members, directing their attention to the role play.

PERFORMANCE FEEDBACK

1. Seek feedback from the coactor, observers, leaders, and main actor in turn.

2. Provide reinforcement at the earliest appropriate opportunity after the role plays.

3. Provide reinforcement to the coactor for being helpful and cooperative.

4. Praise particular aspects of performance (e.g., "You used a brave voice to say that").

5. Provide reinforcement in an amount consistent with the quality of the role play.

TRANSFER TRAINING

1. Assign homework to those who have successfully role played the skill.

2. Discuss completed homework assignments with each child.

3. Provide reinforcement for completing homework assignments.

4. Have the children share their successfully completed homework at the beginning of the next Skillstreaming session.

MAINTENANCE

1. Maintain the behaviors learned by employing individual or group plans to notice and reward skill use. In other words, use self-monitoring, group focus on target skills, Skill Tickets, Skill Notes, awards, and skill folders as appropriate.

CHAPTER 6

Prosocial Skills

This chapter presents the Skillstreaming curriculum, a set of 40 skills designed to enhance the prosocial development of the preschool and kindergarten child. These skills are divided into the following six skill groups: (1) Beginning Social Skills, which are more easily learned by the young child and often are prerequisite to later skill instruction; (2) School-Related Skills, which enhance success primarily in the school or day care environment; (3) Friendship-Making Skills, which encourage positive peer interaction; (4) Dealing with Feelings, which are designed to foster awareness of the feelings of self and others; (5) Alternatives to Aggression, which provide the child with prosocial choices in dealing with conflict; and (6) Dealing with Stress, which address the stressful situations frequently encountered by the young child.

The skills included in this curriculum involve those social behaviors believed to be related to peer acceptance (Dodge, 1983; Greenwood, Todd, Hops, & Walker, 1982; Mize & Ladd, 1984), positive teacher attention (Cartledge & Milburn, 1980), and social competence (Spivack & Shure, 1974), as well as those likely to enhance children's personal satisfaction (Goldstein, Sprafkin, Gershaw, & Klein, 1980). Additional prosocial skills have been selected to teach alternatives to the maladaptive behaviors often employed by unpopular or rejected children, such as poor cooperation (Coie & Kupersmidt, 1983), anxiety (Buhremester, 1982), disruptive behaviors (Dodge, Coie, & Bralke, 1982), and verbal and physical aggression (Dodge et al., 1982).

This list of prosocial behaviors is by no means all-inclusive; instead, our goal is to provide teachers and others who recognize skill deficits in young children with clear and detailed lesson plans to teach the behavioral skills typically needed by preschool and kindergarten children. As the person who implements these plans observes concerns in the school and play environments and as parents and children express difficulties, new skills can and should be developed. For example, although Asking a Question (Skill 9) is intended to encompass asking permission as well, the teacher who finds problems pertaining to asking permission to be frequent may choose to designate and develop this behavior as a separate prosocial skill. In addition, when the individual needs of the children and the circumstances of the setting are considered, it may be that a given skill will be retained but that one or more of the behavioral steps will need to be altered or deleted to achieve the best outcome.

PREREQUISITE SKILLS

The behavioral skills outlined in this chapter are designed for children 3 to 6 years of age and for older children if their development matches that of this younger group. Although most children in this age group will be successful in learning the skills when provided Skillstreaming instruction, the teacher will need to consider a few prerequisites. For example, the child selected should be able to (1) attend to an ongoing activity for a short period of time (approximately 10 minutes); (2) follow simple directions; and (3) understand language concepts such as *same, different, or,* and *not* (Spivack & Shure, 1974). Deficiencies in these competencies will have to be remediated by maturation or direct teacher efforts prior to including the child in a Skillstreaming group. However, the young child with an educational handicap who possesses some of the prerequisites but who perhaps has difficulty attending for this time period in a group setting may benefit from Skillstreaming conducted on an individual basis. Likewise, a child with a language or communication handicap may still be included in the group, with special attention and instruction being given in the areas of concept, sequencing, and so forth.

SELECTION AND SEQUENCE OF SKILLS

We recommend that the teacher initiate instruction with the Beginning Social Skills (Group I). Several of the skills included in this group serve as behavioral steps for later skills or address important facets of skill performance, such as the manner in which a skill is performed. Other skills in this group are frequently needed and will likely bring a positive outcome, thus validating the success of prosocial skill training for children and teacher alike.

Once the children have learned the Group I skills, other skills should be selected on the basis of the needs and problems experienced by the youngsters. Although some children will be eager to discuss areas of skill need for themselves or their peers (e.g., "Megan keeps calling me names, and I get mad. Can we work on that?"), it is often up to the teacher to plan group discussions that will facilitate the sharing of such information. In addition, the children's responses on the Child Skill Checklist (see chap. 3, Figure 3) and the Skill Situations Measure (see chap. 3, Figure 5) can provide valuable information about the skills children feel they need to learn. Because the needs of the group may vary, one or more skills may be selected from each of the remaining five skill groups, the particular sequence of instruction depending on the most critical needs of the majority of youngsters in the group. Allowing youngsters to identify their own areas of skill need and to use skills in ways that benefit them will help promote effective and enduring learning.

After considering the deficits expressed by the children, the teacher can review skills valued by others in the child's environment, such as parents and other teachers. Selection of skills valued in the home and neighborhood can be made easier by considering parents' responses on the Parent Skill Checklist (see chap. 3, Figure 2). Considering parent input in the selection decision may help the teacher identify skills that, although beneficial in the school setting, may actually be contradictory to the expectations of home and neighborhood. Information from the parents can then guide the teacher in emphasizing the specific settings in which a particular skill can be most useful. The teacher can select additional skills by observing difficulties the children are experiencing in following school routines, interacting with classmates, and dealing with stressful or conflict situations. The Teacher Skill Checklist (see chap. 3, Figure 1) can be useful in identifying these problematic areas. Teaching the prosocial skills valued by the children's parents, peers, and teachers increases the likelihood that natural rewards will be forthcoming in the real-life environment. Such rewards may help children maintain their use of the prosocial skills once teaching ceases (Stokes & Baer, 1977).

SKILL AGENDA

Introducing New Skills

To reduce the possible interference of new learning on previously learned material, a second skill should be introduced only when the child can recall the steps of the first skill, has had an opportunity to role play it, and has shown some initial transfer of learning outside of the group teaching setting. Therefore, it may be necessary to spend four or five sessions on one skill. In the case of more complicated skills, 2 or 3 weeks or even longer may be needed before proceeding to yet another skill. Periodic review of previously learned skills can provide the opportunity to reinforce these skills and to encourage their use in new situations, provide systematic fading of the teaching to enhance generalization (Buckley &

Walker, 1978), and prevent boredom that may occur with the concentration on one skill.

Skill Shifting

During instruction in a given prosocial skill, the need frequently arises for training in a different skill. For example, a child who responds with aggression when angry may need to learn not only Dealing with Feeling Mad (Skill 28), but also the skills associated with the factors precipitating his anger, such as Asking for Help (Skill 6) or Dealing with Losing (Skill 36). When such a circumstance occurs, it is important for the teacher to shift to the new skill on the spot or make note of the need to do so in a later session.

SKILL PERFORMANCE

The competent use of prosocial skills is a complex process. Because our goal in teaching such behaviors is for the child to perform the skill in the context of her real-life situation rather than in the isolation of the training setting, several aspects of the skill use context need to be considered. As the work of Dodge (1985) and Spivack and Shure (1974) suggests, for competent skill performance the child should be able to answer the following questions:

1. Why should I use the skill?

2. With whom should I use the skill?

3. What skill should I choose?

4. Where should I use the skill?

5. When should I use the skill?

6. How should I perform the skill?

7. What should I do if the skill is unsuccessful?

Although many of these issues are addressed in the skills themselves as particular behavioral steps and in the four components of Skillstreaming (modeling, role playing, performance feedback, and transfer training), additional emphasis upon these critical aspects can be achieved via group discussion, supplementary role-play practice, and related activities.

Why Should I Use the Skill?

Children will be more likely to learn a new behavior or skill if they are motivated to do so. Understanding how prosocial skill performance will help them meet their needs – get the favor they want or need, stay out of trouble, and so forth – is a valuable aspect in enhancing motivation. Therefore, as the group leaders introduce each skill, they must point out the specific and direct benefits to be gained.

With Whom Should I Use the Skill?

To perform the skill competently, the child must learn to assess and interpret the verbal and nonverbal cues of the person(s) to whom the skill performance is directed. For example, it is sometimes the case that a child who is learning Joining In (Skill 15) fails to assess the receptivity of the target peer group. If the group appears to be avoiding the skill-deficient child (i.e., continuing to move the activity away, refusing to make eye contact, or even shouting at him to go away), the child will need to learn how to attend to such cues and interpret their meaning. The teacher can help by guiding the child in selecting another person or group to approach or in urging a related, back-up skill toward the first group. Likewise, although Saying No (Skill 38) may help avoid a trouble-causing situation when directed toward a friend, the outcome may be quite different if the skill is tried with a parent who is directing the child to get ready for school. Such parameters of skill use may not be easily identified by many young children, and discussions of this issue will need to be an integral part of skill training.

What Skill Should I Choose?

Those involved in Skillstreaming will need to decide which skill should be used in a given situation by anticipating the likely consequences or outcomes of the selected choice. Although one can never be absolutely certain how others will respond to a given overture, children can and should be guided in consequential thinking. Toward this end, the teacher may ask questions such as "How has that person reacted in the past?"; "What would you do if a friend asked you that?"; or "What do you think the result of that might be?" One goal of learning to anticipate the possible consequences of an action is to provide enough relevant information to encourage youngsters to make good choices. Another advantage of teaching this strategy is that it enhances the likelihood that children will stop to think about consequences before actually taking action.

Where Should I Use the Skill?

The skill-deficient child will need help in evaluating the setting in which she intends to use the skill. Using Asking Someone to Play (Skill 19), for instance, may be desirable during classroom free play or during outside recess but would not be encouraged while shopping at the grocery store with a parent. Although adults may assume that most children automatically make this type of determination, this has not proven to be the case. Instead, varied settings in which the skill will likely be successful or unsuccessful should be addressed through group discussion and multiple role plays.

When Should I Use the Skill?

When a skill should be used is often a question for the preschooler or kindergartner. It is not unusual, for example, for the child to use Asking a Question (Skill 9) while the teacher is giving directions or while a parent is involved in an interaction with another child. Therefore, discussions related to the timing of skill use need to be included with each skill.

How Should I Perform the Skill?

The manner in which a youngster performs a skill can determine its effectiveness. For example, a child who uses Asking a Favor (Skill 7) in an angry manner will likely find that the favor will not be granted. Likewise, the child who employs the steps of Dealing with Teasing (Skill 27) but who is obviously upset at being provoked may not find the skill effective. Two behavioral skills to be taught early on therefore deal solely with the manner in which a skill is delivered: Using Nice Talk (Skill 2), to encourage the child to employ a friendly manner, and Using Brave Talk (Skill 3), to encourage the child to make an assertive response.

What Should I Do If the Skill Is Unsuccessful?

Although the training setting is designed to provide for the successful outcome of skill performance, we know that in real life even a highly competent performance may fail to bring about the desired outcome. This failure may be due to inaccurate assessment of the receptivity of the other individuals involved or aspects of the setting such as the degree of structure imposed. Despite the uncontrollability of the world outside the Skillstreaming setting, it is important that the child be rewarded for his attempts whenever possible and that he have repeated practice in making another prosocial skill choice when his initial choice fails. Discussions about the possible reasons for the failure may also be valuable in the child's future skill attempts.

SKILL LESSON PLANS

The latter part of this chapter consists of skill lesson plans for each of the 40 prosocial skills included in the curriculum. Each plan presents the specific behavioral steps that will guide children in skill performance. These behavioral steps are accompanied by simple drawings to help prereading children understand the requested behavior. Notes for discussion also accompany the behavioral steps; these provide additional information about each step and give suggestions for enhancing the effectiveness of skill training. Situations for modeling displays associated with the school, home, and peer group environments are detailed, and additional comments concerning skill performance are included. Finally, ideas for related activities are provided when appropriate.

PROSOCIAL SKILLS

Group I: Beginning Social Skills

1. Listening

2. Using Nice Talk

3. Using Brave Talk

4. Saying Thank You

5. Rewarding Yourself

6. Asking for Help

7. Asking a Favor

8. Ignoring

Group II: School-Related Skills

9. Asking a Question

10. Following Directions

11. Trying When It's Hard

12. Interrupting

Group III: Friendship-Making Skills

13. Greeting Others

14. Reading Others

15. Joining In

16. Waiting Your Turn

17. Sharing

18. Offering Help

19. Asking Someone to Play

20. Playing a Game

Group IV: Dealing with Feelings

21. Knowing Your Feelings

22. Feeling Left Out

23. Asking to Talk

24. Dealing with Fear

25. Deciding How Someone Feels

26. Showing Affection

Group V: Alternatives to Aggression

27. Dealing with Teasing

28. Dealing with Feeling Mad

29. Deciding If It's Fair

30. Solving a Problem

31. Accepting Consequences

Group VI: Dealing with Stress

32. Relaxing

33. Dealing with Mistakes

34. Being Honest

35. Knowing When to Tell

36. Dealing with Losing

37. Wanting to Be First

38. Saying No

39. Accepting No

40. Deciding What to Do

Listening

STEPS

1. **Look.**

   Discuss the importance of looking at the person who is talking. Point out that sometimes you may think someone isn't listening, even though he really is. These steps are to show someone that you are really listening.

2. **Stay still.**

   Remind the children that staying still means keeping hands and feet still and not talking with friends.

3. **Think.**

   Encourage children to think about what the person is saying and be sure they understand if the person is asking them to do something.

SUGGESTED SITUATIONS

   School: Your teacher tells you that you are to go to the art center or gives you instructions on how to do an activity.

   Home: A parent is telling you the plans for the weekend.

Peer group: A friend is telling you a story.

COMMENTS

This is a good skill with which to begin your Skillstreaming group. Adults often tell young children to listen without explaining the specific behaviors or steps necessary to do so. Once the skill of listening is learned, it can be incorporated into classroom rules. Giving the children a special cue to listen (e.g., "Do you have your listening ears on?") may help them apply the skill when needed.

RELATED ACTIVITIES

Play listening games such as Simon Says.

Using Nice Talk

STEPS

1. Use a friendly look.

Discuss how your body and facial expressions can give a friendly or unfriendly look. You may want to act out different facial expressions and body postures to help the children identify what is friendly.

2. Use a friendly voice.

Tell the children that a friendly voice is an "inside" voice – not loud like they might use outside, angry, or whining. Again, you may wish to act out different voice tones and volumes and have the children identify which ones are friendly.

SUGGESTED SITUATIONS

    School: A teacher has asked you to do a favor.

    Home: A parent has just reminded you to clean your room.

Peer group: A friend is playing with the toy you wanted.

COMMENTS

This skill is intended to be used with other skills that require a verbal response. The children can be helped to understand that often it's not so much *what* is said that may elicit an angry response as the *way* it is said. Once children have learned this skill, reminding them to use nice talk can reduce the frequency of talking too loudly and/or whining.

Using Brave Talk

STEPS

1. When?

Discuss situations in which children should use a brave (i.e., assertive) response.

2. Use a brave look.

Discuss body posture and facial expressions that convey a brave look. Distinguish this look from an angry look (e.g., clenching teeth) and a friendly look (e.g., smiling).

3. Use a brave voice.

Discuss that a brave voice is one slightly louder than a friendly one and in which the words are spoken more clearly. Show examples of this voice versus friendly and angry voices.

SUGGESTED SITUATIONS

School: A friend keeps pressuring you to take one of the school toys home with you.

Home: A brother or sister encourages you to draw a picture on the outside of the house with markers.

Peer group: A friend wants you both to play in your parents' car.

COMMENTS

Another situation in which children could use this skill is when an older peer urges them to behave in ways that make them feel uncomfortable (e.g., crossing the street when they are not supposed to). The use of puppets may help to lessen the child's anxiety when role playing such situations.

RELATED ACTIVITIES

Spend time showing different expressions and tones of voice to the children by using pictures, videotapes, and/or performing the actions live. Have the children hold up cards to indicate if the actions are friendly, brave, or angry.

Saying Thank You

STEPS

1. Was it nice to do?

Talk about nice things that parents, teachers, and friends do for others. Tell the children that saying thank you is a way to let someone know you are happy about what that person did for you.

2. When?

Discuss appropriate times to say thank you (i.e., when the person isn't busy).

3. Say "Thank you."

Let the children know that they may want to tell the person why they are saying thank you (e.g., that they really wanted that toy or that something the person did made them feel good), especially if they must thank the person later.

SUGGESTED SITUATIONS

School: Someone gives you a school toy that you wanted.

Home: A parent fixes your favorite dinner.

Peer group: A friend invites you to a birthday party or lets you play with a special toy.

COMMENTS

The children may generate other ways to say thank you, such as smiling, giving a hug, or doing something nice for the person. It may be useful to practice different ways of saying thank you, such as "That was nice of you to do for me" or "I felt good when you said that to me." If children have already learned Using Nice Talk (Skill 2), they can be reminded to do so when they are saying thanks.

RELATED ACTIVITIES

Have the children make pictures of all the people in the school or community who have helped them and then decide how the class could thank them. Carry out these plans.

Rewarding Yourself

STEPS

1. How did you do?

Discuss ways of evaluating one's own performance. These might include feeling as though something was hard but that you tried, hearing someone else praise your efforts, or having a good feeling inside about how you did.

2. Say "Good for me!"

Discuss the feeling of being proud of yourself. Have the children talk about times when they have felt this way. Give examples of other things they might say to reward themselves (e.g., "Way to go," "I did really well," etc.).

SUGGESTED SITUATIONS

School: You helped the teacher or another child or did a good job on an activity.

Home: You cleaned up your room or helped to clear the table.

Peer group: You helped a friend learn how to play a game.

COMMENTS

Emphasize that a person doesn't always have to depend on others to reward her actions.

RELATED ACTIVITIES

At the end of the day, let each child tell you about one accomplishment. Write a note to the child's parents about the achievement.

Asking for Help

STEPS

1. **Try it.**

   Talk about the importance of trying on your
   own first: Sometimes people ask for help instead
   of trying something difficult by themselves, but
   doing something difficult on your own can give
   people a feeling of pride.

2. **Say "I need help."**

   Acknowledge that sometimes it's frustrating
   when something is difficult to do, but stress the
   importance of Using Nice Talk (Skill 2). The
   child may also want to use Saying Thank You
   (Skill 4) after the help is given.

SUGGESTED SITUATIONS

   School: You need help putting the paints back up on the shelf.

   Home: You need help from a parent in getting dressed for
   school or finding your swimming suit.

Peer group: You want to ask a friend to help you learn to ride
   your bike.

RELATED ACTIVITIES

Have the children list and/or illustrate the activities each is particularly
good at. Discuss individual differences; stress that it is OK to ask for
help if it's needed. These lists may also stimulate the children to ask for
help from peers who have listed certain areas as strengths.

Asking a Favor

STEPS

1. What do you want?

Explain that this skill may be used to express children's wants or needs but that the favor should be a fair one. Deciding If It's Fair (Skill 29) will help determine this.

2. Plan what to say.

Talk about the importance of planning what to say and suggest several possible ways to ask. The children may also want to give a reason for asking the favor (e.g., "Could you please move a little? I can't see when you sit there.").

3. Ask.

Remind the children of the importance of Using Nice Talk (Skill 2).

4. Say "Thank you."

Refer to Saying Thank You (Skill 4).

SUGGESTED SITUATIONS

School: You want to use the markers another child is using.

Home: You ask your parent to make popcorn.

Peer group: You want to ride a friend's bicycle.

COMMENTS

Once the children have been successful in using this skill in role-play situations, it is particularly important that they practice what to do when the favor isn't granted. Adding the statement "Thanks anyway" or having the child get involved in something else may be helpful.

RELATED ACTIVITIES

Make a list of favors that would be fair and those that would not. For example, if a person has a pack of gum, would it be fair to ask for a piece? If a person has one stick of gum, would it be fair to ask for it?

Ignoring

STEPS

1. Look away.

Tell the children not to look at the person they want to avoid. They can turn their heads away, look at a friend, or pick up a book or toy to look at.

2. Close your ears.

Tell children not to listen to what the other person is saying. If they are supposed to be listening to someone else, they can listen to that person.

3. Be quiet.

Remind children not to say anything back to the person who is annoying them.

SUGGESTED SITUATIONS

School: Another child is talking when you are supposed to be listening to the teacher.

Home: A brother or sister is trying to keep you from listening to your record.

Peer group: Another child is trying to interfere with a game you are playing.

COMMENTS

Discuss the fact that sometimes someone who is acting silly is trying to get attention. A good way to teach that person not to act silly is to avoid giving him any attention at all. Also discuss the idea that sometimes friends will bother others because they really want to play, too. In this case, the children may want to ask the child to join in. Finally, talk about other ways of ignoring, such as leaving the room at home or getting involved in another activity at school.

Asking a Question

STEPS

1. What to ask?

Discuss what children need to ask and how to decide whether the question is really necessary. Help them plan out what they need to ask.

2. Whom to ask?

Discuss how to decide if they should ask the teacher, a parent, or someone else.

3. When to ask?

Talk about how to choose a good time to ask (i.e., when the other person isn't busy).

4. Ask.

Stress the importance of Using Nice Talk (Skill 2).

SUGGESTED SITUATIONS

School: You want to ask your teacher about when the field trip is or whether you can play with a certain toy.

Home: You want to ask a parent if you can visit a friend.

Peer group: You want to ask a friend if she would like to play at your house or how she made something.

COMMENTS

Young children often phrase questions as statements. Modeling the question form when such situations arise will help them learn an alternate way of expressing themselves.

RELATED ACTIVITIES

Practice asking questions via a game format. For example, make a statement such as "I want a glass of milk" and ask the children to change the statement to a question (i.e., "May I have a glass of milk?"). State a topic (e.g., swimming) and generate several questions that could be asked about that topic. Discourage unrelated questions.

Following Directions

STEPS

1. Listen.

Review Listening (Skill 1). Discuss the importance of having children show that they are listening.

2. Think about it.

Remind the children to think about what is being said.

3. Ask if needed.

Encourage children to ask questions about anything that they don't understand.

4. Do it.

SUGGESTED SITUATIONS

School: Your teacher gives you the directions to do some work at a learning center.

Home: A parent gives you directions to make a snack.

Peer group: A friend tells you how to play a game.

COMMENTS

Sometimes directions given to young children are too complex for them to complete successfully. Give directions consisting of only one or two steps until the children are familiar with following directions. It's helpful to preface a direction with a consistent cue, such as "Here's the direction."

RELATED ACTIVITIES

Play the Treasure Hunt game, giving the children verbal directions to find a special treat or activity (e.g., "Walk to the bookshelf and look on the bottom shelf under the big book").

Trying When It's Hard

STEPS

1. Stop and think.

Discuss the feeling of frustration and point out that lots of people get frustrated when something is difficult.

2. Say "It's hard, but I'll try."

Talk about feeling proud when something is hard but you try it anyway. Also stress that it's OK to try and fail.

3. Try it.

Point out that a person might need to try more than once.

SUGGESTED SITUATIONS

School: Your teacher gives you an activity that you don't think you can do.

Home: A parent wants you to do a chore that you don't think you can do (e.g., make the beds).

Peer group: A friend wants you to roller skate with him, but you think it's too hard.

COMMENTS

For the child who is afraid of failure, this will be a particularly valuable skill. Reinforce that the only way to learn new things is to try those that are difficult. When assigning preacademic or academic skills, be sure that tasks asked of the children are ones they are capable of completing with effort.

RELATED ACTIVITIES

Read *The Little Engine That Could,* by Watty Piper (1976), and discuss the feelings of each of the characters in the story. Also discuss what might have happened if the little engine didn't try. (Stories with similar themes can be substituted.)

Interrupting

STEPS

1. **Decide if you need to.**

   Discuss when it is appropriate to interrupt (i.e., when you need help but the person you want to talk to isn't looking at you).

2. **Walk to the person.**

3. **Wait.**

   Emphasize the importance of waiting without talking. Tell children to wait until the person stops talking and looks at you.

4. **Say "Excuse me."**

   After saying this, children can then ask what they need to ask.

SUGGESTED SITUATIONS

School: Your teacher is talking with another adult, and you need help with your activity.

Home: A parent is talking on the telephone, and you want to ask whether you can go outside.

Peer group: Your friend is talking with another person, and you want to ask whether you can play with your friend's wagon.

COMMENTS

It will be important to discuss situations in which children should not interrupt (e.g., to ask a question that could wait) and situations in which they should interrupt immediately (i.e., in an emergency). It may be helpful to have the children actually say to the adult, "This is an emergency" when such cases arise.

RELATED ACTIVITIES

Provide pictures of a variety of situations and, as a group, have the children put the pictures under the headings *Do Not Interrupt, OK to Interrupt,* or *Emergency.*

Greeting Others

STEPS

1. Smile.

2. Say "Hi, _____."

Encourage children to use the person's name if they know it.

3. Walk on.

This step should be used if the children are supposed to be following along with the group or if they don't know the person well. The children may wish to begin a conversation if the person is a friend.

SUGGESTED SITUATIONS

School: You pass by the school secretary in the hallway.

Home: A friend of your parents is visiting.

Peer group: Another child is walking past your house with her parents.

COMMENTS

This skill is intended to be used with people known only casually by the child or in situations in which starting a conversation would be inappropriate.

RELATED ACTIVITIES

Take a walk around the school and practice greeting others.

Reading Others

STEPS

1. Look at the face.

Discuss the importance of watching for different facial expressions, such as smiling, frowning, clenching teeth together, and so forth.

2. Look at the body.

Talk about the feelings shown in a person's body position, such as putting head down, making fists with hands, placing hands on hips, and so on.

SUGGESTED SITUATIONS

School: The teacher walks in the class and smiles, or she has her hands on her hips and frowns.

Home: A parent is sitting with his head resting on his hands and not saying anything.

Peer group: A friend keeps turning away from you and doesn't answer you when you try to talk.

COMMENTS

This skill, which concentrates on learning to pay attention to body language, should be taught before teaching Joining In (Skill 15) and Deciding How Someone Feels (Skill 25). This skill will help children assess the receptivity of those to whom they are directing skill use.

Joining In

STEPS

1. Move closer.

Point out that the children should be fairly close to where the activity is taking place.

2. Watch.

Tell the children to watch the ongoing activity and wait for a pause. Discuss the importance of choosing a good time to follow through with the next step (i.e., before the activity has begun or when there is a break in the activity).

3. Ask.

Suggest possible things to say, such as "That looks fun! Could I play, too?" Stress the importance of Using Brave Talk (Skill 3).

SUGGESTED SITUATIONS

School: You want to join in a game at recess or during free play.

Home: You want to play a game with a brother, sister, or parent.

Peer group: You want to join a group of children at the park.

COMMENTS

Research indicates that attempts to join in are more successful if the child hovers near the ongoing activity before asking to join in (Dodge, Schlundt, Schoken, & Dehugach, 1983). Children may need to use alternative skills if they are repeatedly rejected by a certain peer group. Practice in Reading Others (Skill 14) may help them assess other children's receptivity to such overtures.

Waiting Your Turn

STEPS

1. Say "It's hard to wait, but I can do it."

Discuss how the children feel when they have to wait.

2. Choose.

a. Wait quietly.

Discuss that this choice means not talking or bothering anyone else and remembering not to get angry or frustrated.

b. Do something else.

Talk about what things the children could do while they are waiting.

3. Do it.

Children should make one of these choices.

SUGGESTED SITUATIONS

School: You are waiting your turn to play a game or to use the playground equipment.

Home: You are waiting until it's time for you to go to a movie or the park.

Peer group: You are waiting your turn to have a toy.

RELATED ACTIVITIES

To practice this skill, as well as to show the group a product resulting from working together and taking turns, you may want to structure round-robin activities in the classroom, such as cooperatively making a collage or putting together a puzzle.

Sharing

STEPS

1. Make a sharing plan.

Discuss the different plans children could make, such as playing with a toy together or having each child take a turn with the toy for a set period of time.

2. Ask.

Remind the children of the importance of Using Nice Talk (Skill 2) when asking friends if they agree to the plan.

3. Do it.

Talk about the importance of following through with the plan until a different plan is decided upon.

SUGGESTED SITUATIONS

School: You have to share the paste and other art materials with two other children.

Home: You must share the last popsicle with a brother or sister.

Peer group: You have to share your toys with a friend who has come to your house to play.

COMMENTS

It is appropriate to discuss how the children feel when someone doesn't share with them and to encourage them to think about their feelings when someone asks them to share.

RELATED ACTIVITIES

Plan activities to encourage this skill, such as sharing art materials, taking turns when cooking, or engaging in other cooperative activities.

Offering Help

STEPS

1. Decide if someone needs help.

Discuss how to tell when someone might want or need help (e.g., someone has lots to carry or is showing frustration).

2. Ask.

Discuss appropriate ways of asking, such as saying, "May I help you?" or "How can I help you?"

3. Do it.

SUGGESTED SITUATIONS

School: Your teacher looks frustrated while trying to pass out snacks and help a child who is upset at the same time.

Home: A parent is hurrying to get dinner ready.

Peer group: A friend is having trouble getting her coat on.

COMMENTS

Discuss what to do if the person doesn't want the help (e.g., walk away, get involved in another activity, say to yourself, "I did a good job asking" or "It was nice of me to ask").

RELATED ACTIVITIES

Include this skill when teaching units on community helpers by asking the people who come in to talk to the class to discuss ways they offer help to others.

Asking Someone to Play

STEPS

1. Decide if you want to.

Discuss how to decide whether you want
someone to play with or would rather play
alone. Point out that there might be times when
you would rather be alone.

2. Decide who.

Talk about whom the child might choose (e.g.,
someone who is playing alone, someone new in
the class the child would like to get to know, or
someone who isn't busy).

3. Ask.

Discuss and practice ways to ask.

SUGGESTED SITUATIONS

School: You want to play with someone when it's free play
time.

Home: You want to ask a brother, sister, or parent to play.

Peer group: You want to play with a friend in the neighborhood.

COMMENTS

It is important to point out that it is best to ask someone to play after
he has finished his work at school or home.

Playing a Game

STEPS

1. Know the rules.

Discuss that everyone playing should agree on the rules before the game is begun.

2. Who goes first?

Talk about ways to decide, such as rolling a die or offering to let the other person go first.

3. Wait for a turn.

Emphasize the importance of paying attention to the game and watching and waiting for your own turn.

SUGGESTED SITUATIONS

School: You are practicing shooting baskets at recess with two other friends.

Home: You are playing Candy Land with your mom and dad.

Peer group: You are playing school with a friend.

COMMENTS

Two good skills to teach along with this one are Dealing with Losing (Skill 36) and Wanting to Be First (Skill 37).

RELATED ACTIVITIES

Provide opportunities for the children to play board games in pairs or small groups, emphasizing use of this skill. Teach a variety of games children may play at recess or during free play in the classroom.

Knowing Your Feelings

STEPS

1. **Think about what happened.**

   Discuss what happened that may have caused the feeling. Also talk about the signals the children's bodies give that indicate they are having a strong feeling.

2. **Decide on the feeling.**

   Discuss a variety of feelings, such as anger, happiness, frustration, fear, and so on.

3. **Say "I feel** _____."**

SUGGESTED SITUATIONS

   School: You have to go to a new school, where you don't know any of the kids.

   Home: Your parent announces that the whole family is going to Disneyland.

Peer group: You didn't get invited to a friend's birthday party.

COMMENTS

Explore as many different feeling words as the children can handle, trying to expand their vocabulary from the typical feelings of happy, sad, and mad.

RELATED ACTIVITIES

Read stories that describe feelings, such as *I Was So Mad,* by Mercer Mayer (1983), or *Feelings,* by Joanne Murphy (1985). Present pictures and help children identify what feelings may be expressed and generate ideas as to what may have caused these feelings.

Feeling Left Out

STEPS

1. Decide what happened.

Discuss situations in which the children may feel left out and help them decide what caused them to feel this way. Talk about reasons why someone may not be included (e.g., a friend could only invite three people to her birthday party).

2. Choose.

a. Join in.

Children will need prior instruction in Joining In (Skill 15).

b. Do something else.

Generate ideas for other things children could do. Suggest that they may want to invite a friend to do one of these activities.

3. Do it.

Children should make one of these choices.

SUGGESTED SITUATIONS

School: You are left out of a game during free play.

Home: Your sister won't let you come in her room.

Peer group: A friend has invited someone else to go skating.

COMMENTS

The children may need practice in Reading Others (Skill 14) or Deciding How Someone Feels (Skill 25) in order to assess whether or not the other child or group of children is approachable.

RELATED ACTIVITIES

Discuss the types of feelings that result from being left out, such as anger, hurt, or frustration.

Asking to Talk

STEPS

1. Decide if you need to talk.

Discuss times when something might bother children and they might want to talk to someone about it. Such times might occur when they feel sad or need help solving a problem.

2. Who?

Decide whom to talk with (i.e., a parent, teacher, or friend).

3. When?

Decide when would be a good time to ask (i.e., when the person isn't busy with something or someone else).

4. Say "I need to talk."

Stress the importance of Using Nice Talk (Skill 2) to say this.

SUGGESTED SITUATIONS

School: You are feeling sad because you didn't get to have a turn at the painting center.

Home: You feel that your parents aren't spending as much time with you as you'd like.

Peer group: You feel that a friend would rather play with someone other than you.

COMMENTS

Stress that everyone experiences problems at some time and, although talking with someone may not actually solve the problem, it may help make you feel better anyway.

Dealing with Fear

STEPS

1. What?

Discuss situations that cause children to be afraid.

2. Choose.

a. Ask to talk.

Refer to Asking to Talk (Skill 23).

b. Relax.

Refer to Relaxing (Skill 32).

3. Do it.

Children should make one of these choices.

SUGGESTED SITUATIONS

School: A parent is late, and you're afraid she isn't coming.

Home: A brother or sister is watching a scary movie.

Peer group: You are afraid to go out of the house because an older child said he would get you.

COMMENTS

Discuss the fact that there are events in which a real danger is present and fear is appropriate. Many other situations, such as being afraid of the dark, are quite normal for this age group and likely present no serious problems for most children. However, explain that sometimes we may be afraid to try new things; in this case, the children should be encouraged to use Trying When It's Hard (Skill 11) after first using one of the choices listed in this skill.

Deciding How Someone Feels

STEPS

1. **Watch the person.**

   Discuss a variety of feelings, such as frustration, anger, happiness, fear, and so on. Help children describe the kinds of body language and words that correspond to these feelings.

2. **Name the feeling.**

3. **Ask.**

   Decide whether to ask the person if he is feeling this way or whether to do something to help that person. If the person seems very angry or upset, point out that it may be best to wait until he is calm.

SUGGESTED SITUATIONS

   School: A large jar of paint was spilled on a child, and she has started to cry.

   Home: A parent has dropped a sack of groceries, and he is shaking his head and sighing.

Peer group: A friend of yours asked someone to play, but the person said no.

COMMENTS

This skill extends Reading Others (Skill 14) to include the verbal expression of feelings. Children might also be encouraged to use Offering Help (Skill 18) following this skill if the circumstances warrant.

Showing Affection

STEPS

1. Decide if you have nice feelings.

Discuss how to decide if you have positive feelings about someone. Talk about the people children might want to show affection toward (friends, parents, and teachers versus strangers).

2. Choose.

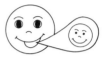

a. Say it.

Talk about things the children might say to friends, parents, or teachers.

b. Hug.

c. Do something.

Discuss nice things that could be done for someone to show caring.

3. When?

Talk about appropriate times to show affection.

4. Do it.

Children should make one of these choices.

SUGGESTED SITUATIONS

School: You want to show your teacher that you like her.

Home: You want to show affection to your grandparents.

Peer group: You want to let a friend know that you like him.

COMMENTS

Because several choices are included in this skill, it may be a difficult one for some younger preschoolers. If so, limit the choices. Some children will need additional help to distinguish between people known well and comparative strangers. Greeting Others (Skill 13) can be suggested for use with people known less well.

Dealing with Teasing

STEPS

1. Stop and think.

Discuss the importance of giving yourself time before reacting and the likely consequences of saying something back or acting aggressive. Talk about the reasons people tease (to get others mad or to get their attention).

2. Say "Please stop."

Stress the importance of Using Brave Talk (Skill 3) and practice this skill.

3. Walk away.

This step is important to help end the teasing situation. After walking away, the child may need to use other skills, such as Asking to Talk (Skill 23) or Relaxing (Skill 32).

SUGGESTED SITUATIONS

School: On the playground, someone is calling you a name.

Home: A brother or sister tells you something that you know isn't true, such as your face is blue or you're going out to dinner when you know you're not.

Peer group: A friend is teasing you that she can ride a bike better than you can.

COMMENTS

It may be important for the young child to talk with another friend or adult about the teasing.

Dealing with Feeling Mad

STEPS

1. Stop and think.

Discuss the importance of stopping and not doing anything. Talk about the consequences of acting out this feeling in a negative way (e.g., hitting the person). Also discuss that stopping and thinking give a person time to make choices.

2. Choose.

a. Turtle.

Instruct children to act like turtles, curling up in their shells where they can't see the person with whom they are angry.

b. Relax.

Refer to Relaxing (Skill 32).

c. Ask to talk.

Discuss people children can talk to. Refer to Asking to Talk (Skill 23) as needed.

3. Do it.

Children should make one of these choices.

SUGGESTED SITUATIONS

School: The teacher won't let you have free play.

Home: It's raining, and a parent won't let you ride your bike.

Peer group: A friend has taken your basketball and won't give it back.

COMMENTS

It is important to offer children a choice involving a physical response, such as relaxing or doing the turtle. The turtle technique is taken from Schneider and Robin's (1974) *Turtle Manual*.

RELATED ACTIVITIES

Read the story and do the activities included in the *Turtle Manual*.

Deciding If It's Fair

STEPS

1. Think about how the other person feels.

Discuss thinking about how the other person might feel in a situation that isn't fair (e.g., if the teacher always chooses one child to help). Talk about how children feel when they perceive things that aren't fair.

2. What can you do?

Decide if there is anything that could be done to make the situation more fair (e.g., sharing).

3. Do it.

SUGGESTED SITUATIONS

School: You or another child has asked the teacher to play with the scooter that someone else is using.

Home: Both you and your brother or sister want to watch different programs on TV, and your parent says you can watch your program.

Peer group: You want to let another friend play, but the child you're playing with doesn't want the other friend to play, too.

COMMENTS

It is very important that the children begin to understand that things can't always be fair. For example, it might rain when you'd planned to go to the beach, or you might get the flu and have to stay home from the skating party at school.

RELATED ACTIVITIES

For more information about evaluating situations in terms of fairness, see Camp and Bash's (1981, 1985) Think Aloud Program.

Solving a Problem

STEPS

1. Decide on the problem.

Children may need help in defining the problem.

2. Think of choices.

Generate different alternatives children could choose and discuss the likely consequences of each choice.

3. Make a plan.

Decide on one choice to try and plan how to do this.

4. Do it.

SUGGESTED SITUATIONS

School: You have trouble following the teacher's directions.

Home: You have a problem going to bed on time.

Peer group: You like playing with one friend but get upset when another friend comes over to play, too.

COMMENTS

As problems arise in the classroom, lead the class in a discussion of the issues involved and follow these skill steps to implement the plan. Remind children that if one plan doesn't work, they may need to make another plan.

RELATED ACTIVITIES

Have children generate a plan for solving a real-life problem and draw a picture of the plan to share with parents and to save as a reminder to themselves.

Accepting Consequences

STEPS

1. **Stop and think.**

   Stress that this step will give children time to calm down and follow the rest of the steps.

   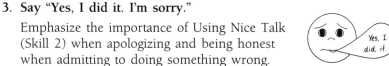

2. **Decide if you're wrong.**

   Discuss that it's OK for children to be wrong.

3. **Say "Yes, I did it. I'm sorry."**

   Emphasize the importance of Using Nice Talk (Skill 2) when apologizing and being honest when admitting to doing something wrong.

4. **Follow the direction.**

   Explain that children may need to do something to resolve the problem (e.g., clean up a mess or help pay for something they broke).

SUGGESTED SITUATIONS

      School: You spilled another child's glass of juice.

      Home: You broke something of your parents.

Peer group: You took a friend's toy without asking permission.

COMMENTS

Some children may have difficulty verbally admitting their behavior or saying they are sorry. If so, this step could be deleted or another step (perhaps shaking your head yes) could be substituted.

Relaxing

STEPS

1. **Think about how you feel.**

   Talk about how children feel when they are
   tense (jittery inside, getting a stomachache, tight
   or warm all over, etc.).

2. **Take three deep breaths.**

   Teach the children how to take relaxing breaths:
   Take a big breath in slowly, then let the air out
   through an open mouth. Have everyone practice
   this step.

3. **Squeeze the oranges.**

   Pretend to give each child an orange in each
   hand. Have children tighten their fists to
   squeeze all the juice out of each orange in turn,
   then both oranges together. Finally, have them
   drop the oranges and shake the rest of the juice
   off their hands.

SUGGESTED SITUATIONS

   School: You are putting on an important puppet show for
   another class.

   Home: You are going on vacation and you're excited, or a
   parent seems angry with you and you don't know
   why.

Peer group: You are waiting to go to a friend's birthday party.

COMMENTS

Children may need a great deal of training in relaxation before they will
be able to use this skill effectively. Having them practice this skill each
day before rest time may help them to fall asleep more easily.

Dealing with Mistakes

STEPS

1. Say "It's OK to make mistakes. Everybody makes mistakes."

Discuss mistakes that you have made. Encourage the children to talk about mistakes they have made. Use humor, if appropriate.

2. Plan for next time.

Have children plan how they could avoid making the same mistakes again. Ideas might include taking more time, asking for help, asking a question, and so on.

SUGGESTED SITUATIONS

School: You make a mistake on an art project.

Home: You make a mistake while helping your parent with cooking.

Peer group: You invited a friend over but forgot to ask your parent's permission.

COMMENTS

Discuss how making a plan before engaging in a difficult task may help prevent mistakes and encourage each child to make such a plan. Because the skill does not require the child to take immediate action, it will be helpful to post the plan in the classroom or at home so that the child will have easy reference to it when needed. (Use pictures to illustrate plans for prereaders.)

RELATED ACTIVITIES

Have everyone who wants to (including the teacher and co-leader) share "most embarrassing moments."

Being Honest

STEPS

1. Think of what can happen.

Help children construct lists of likely consequences of telling and not telling the truth. Also discuss how being honest can sometimes be hurtful (e.g., saying you don't like a person's haircut).

2. Decide to tell the truth.

Discuss how punishing consequences are usually less severe if a person is honest at the start.

3. Say it.

Discuss and practice examples of telling the truth, such as "I'm sorry, but I did it" or "Yes, but I didn't mean to." Emphasize Using Nice Talk (Skill 2).

SUGGESTED SITUATIONS

School: You accidentally broke one of the school's toys.

Home: You hit your brother or sister when you were angry or went across the street without permission.

Peer group: You said something about a friend that was true but not very nice.

COMMENTS

Children should be rewarded for telling the truth, even though there may be other negative consequences for their actions. Encourage children to use Rewarding Yourself (Skill 5) for being honest.

RELATED ACTIVITIES

Spend time discussing the difference between "tall tales" and being dishonest. Read the story of Paul Bunyan and explain that this is a tall tale. Have the children make up their own tall tales. Later, if a child's honesty is questionable, it's OK to ask if he is telling a tall tale.

Knowing When to Tell

STEPS

1. Decide if someone will get hurt.

Explain that children need to decide if the action is likely to hurt the person involved, themselves, or someone else.

2. Whom should you tell?

If the action will not result in someone's getting hurt (e.g., one child's taking a toy from another), the child should talk to the person with whom she has the problem, perhaps using Asking a Favor (Skill 7) or Dealing with Teasing (Skill 27) as needed. If the action will cause harm, the child should tell a teacher, parent, or other responsible adult immediately.

3. Do it.

This should be done in a helpful, friendly way.

SUGGESTED SITUATIONS

School: Someone threatens to hit you or takes your crayons without asking.

Home: A brother or sister is playing with matches.

Peer group: A friend won't share her candy with you.

COMMENTS

This skill is designed to help children know when to involve an adult in a problem and when to attempt to deal with the problem themselves. Toward this end, discuss different types of things that cause hurt to others, such as hitting, pinching, inappropriate touching, or excessive tickling. Even when no actual harm will be done, children should feel free to approach adults to discuss ways of dealing with a problem or to talk about the feelings associated with a situation. These are positive behaviors; what is negative is tattling. If a child does approach you about minor peer conflicts, a helpful response is "How can I help you deal with that?"

Dealing with Losing

STEPS

1. **Say "Everybody can't win."**

   Point out the absurdity of having everyone win a game. Affirm that it is normal to feel disappointed at not winning; discuss the feelings that children have when they don't win.

2. **Say "Maybe I'll win next time."**

   Children should be encouraged to say this in a hopeful, coping manner.

3. **Do something else.**

   Point out that although it's OK to feel disappointed, continuing to think about the disappointment may only cause children to have a bad time.

SUGGESTED SITUATIONS

   School: Your group loses at Duck-Duck-Goose.

   Home: You didn't win when playing a game with a brother, sister, or parent.

Peer group: You came in second in a running race with a friend.

COMMENTS

Cooperative games and activities such as those described by Johnson and Johnson (1986) have been found to teach more positive skills than do competitive activities. When possible, cooperative activities, versus competitive ones, should be included in the school curriculum.

Wanting to Be First

STEPS

1. **Say "Everybody can't be first."**

   Discuss how the children feel when they are first and when they aren't first. Talk about how impossible it would be for everyone to be first.

2. **Say "It's OK not to be first."**

3. **Stay with it.**

   Talk about what children would miss if they quit the activity because they weren't first (i.e., the pleasure of playing a game or being a part of an activity).

SUGGESTED SITUATIONS

School: You're not first in line for recess or lunch.

Home: A brother or sister gets to sit in the front seat on the way to the park, but you have to wait until the ride home.

Peer group: A friend gets to be first when playing a game.

RELATED ACTIVITIES

Many teachers of preschoolers or kindergartners find it helpful to initiate a "child of the week" program in which one child is chosen to share things about himself, such as pictures and special toys, and gets to be the line leader and first at special activities. Other teachers choose children to perform specific classroom duties and to be the line leader on a daily basis. Such activities tend to diminish the frequency of children's distress at not being first.

Saying No

STEPS

1. Decide if you want to do it.

The child needs to decide whether or not
she wants to do what is being asked. Discuss
situations when saying no is appropriate
and when it is not.

2. If not, why not?

The child should think about his reasons for
not wanting to do this (e.g., wanting to do
something else or feeling it might cause trouble
or unnecessarily hurt someone else's feelings).

3. Say "No."

Stress the importance of Using Nice Talk
(Skill 2) when saying no. Point out that the
child might also want to give the reason for
saying no.

SUGGESTED SITUATIONS

School: A friend wants you to leave the classroom.

Home: A younger brother or sister wants you to stay home
and play, but you want to play at a friend's house.

Peer group: A friend wants you to go to the park, but you want to
go swimming with another friend.

COMMENTS

Most situations will require Using Nice Talk (Skill 2). However, if a child
is being pressured to do something she knows is wrong, Using Brave
Talk (Skill 3) would be more appropriate.

Accepting No

STEPS

1. Stop and think.

Discuss the possible reasons children might be told no in various situations.

2. Choose.

a. Do something else.

Discuss the fact that even though you are told you can't do or have something, you can still have fun by doing something else.

b. Ask to talk.

Stress that children can use Asking to Talk (Skill 23) if they do not understand the reason for being told no. However, point out that Using Nice Talk (Skill 2) is very important, or the parent or teacher may interpret their questions as arguing. Discuss that the goal of asking is to better understand the adult's decision, not to have the adult change the decision.

3. Do it.

Children should make one of these choices.

SUGGESTED SITUATIONS

School: A teacher tells you that it's time to do art and that you can't have free play.

Home: A parent tells you that it's too late to go to a friend's house to play or that you can't get a toy at the grocery store.

Peer group: A friend tells you that he can't play today or won't let you play with one of his toys.

COMMENTS

This skill may be difficult for many young children to accomplish; many practice sessions should be planned.

Deciding What to Do

STEPS

1. Think about what you like to do.

Help the children generate lists of things they like to do that would be acceptable in different situations.

2. Decide on one thing.

3. Do it.

SUGGESTED SITUATIONS

School: It's free play time.

Home: It's a rainy afternoon, and everyone in the house is busy.

Peer group: You and a friend can't think of anything to do.

COMMENTS

After children successfully complete this skill, you may want to encourage them to use Rewarding Yourself (Skill 5).

RELATED ACTIVITIES

Have children make pictures of activities they enjoy on index cards and place them in a card file box under the headings *Home, School,* and *Outdoors.* When children complain of not having anything to do, they can consult their own personal card files.

CHAPTER 7

Managing Behavior Problems

The management of behavior problems is often a challenge in any group teaching endeavor. This chapter will describe a variety of management techniques for use with typical problem behaviors encountered during Skillstreaming instruction, such as inattention, talking out, distracting peers, and leaving the group.

Once a management problem has been identified, the task becomes to select and implement one or more techniques to foster more desirable behavior. We do not suggest that only certain techniques be used with a specific type of problematic behavior. Just as one type of reinforcer may be rewarding for one child but not for another, a particular management strategy is likely to be more effective for one child than for another. Therefore, we will describe a range of strategies to be used when conducting Skillstreaming groups and urge that teachers individualize these methods, using those techniques that appear to work best with given children.

Suggested strategies for managing behavioral concerns are described in the following three sections. The first section provides a six-step plan designed to deal effectively with a wide range of problematic behaviors. The second section offers suggestions for implementing an individual management plan designed to increase the children's positive behaviors. The third section addresses relationship-based techniques.

A SIX-STEP MANAGEMENT PLAN

The following plan provides teachers with a basic format for managing the minor behavioral concerns that may arise on a daily basis. This plan is not intended for use with more severe behaviors for which immediate consequences must be provided (e.g., aggression). If the plan is to be successful, the six steps must be used in sequence.

Step 1: Provide Structure

Many behavior problems can be averted by providing children with a structured environment in which to work and play. Structuring the learning environment includes considering the physical arrangement of the room, planning a schedule or routine for the day, and defining teacher expectations (i.e., classroom rules or guidelines for behavior).

Physical structure

The physical environment can structure the learning setting. Most preschool and kindergarten classrooms have areas designed for a variety of free play activities (e.g., a kitchen center, a play store, art area, etc.) as well as spaces for large group and small group activities. As described in chapter 4, a specific space for conducting Skillstreaming instruction needs to be provided. To minimize potential behavior problems, this area should be large enough so children can participate in role plays without disrupting other group participants. Chairs or carpet samples for the children to sit on may be provided to create physical distance between the children. To reduce distractions, enticing activities such as sand or water tables should be out of the group's view. The group rules, or behavioral guidelines, should be posted as a reminder for the entire group to use positive behavior. In the classroom in general, allowing spaces for traffic can minimize the disruption of ongoing activities as a child moves from one area to another.

Increasing the physical structure of the group setting or classroom can minimize and avert many behavior problems; this structure can then be gradually lessened as the children become more familiar with working together.

Schedules or routines

The teacher should provide a structure for the school day by creating a schedule of events that will take place. Within this schedule, the teacher sets the time for group instruction in Skillstreaming and plans opportunities for the children to practice those prosocial skills they have learned in the formal group setting. For example, if Waiting Your Turn (Skill 16) has been targeted, activities in which the children will need to wait their turn, such as completing a puzzle as a group or drawing a group picture, can be planned. Most preschool and kindergarten teachers find it most helpful to follow the same general schedule each day. Although special activities such as field trips may occasionally alter this general schedule, children at this young age may feel more secure when they have a general daily routine. Providing a schedule of the school day in picture format and reviewing this schedule at the beginning of the day can help to avoid many of the problems associated with a change in routine.

Structure in the form of routine should be provided in the Skillstreaming sessions as well. Although most young children quickly learn the pattern of activities included in Skillstreaming, it is helpful at the beginning of each session to inform the children of the activities that will be taking place (e.g., "We'll show you the skill of Waiting Your Turn, then some of you will get a chance to try it"). Letting the children know which activities they will be participating in will help to prepare them for learning.

Group guidelines

Communicating the teacher's expectations is a critical aspect of providing structure. This is most clearly and easily done by establishing group guidelines or rules for acceptable behavior. Such rules should be reasonable ones that inform the children of what to do rather than forbidding unacceptable behaviors. For example, if no hitting is allowed, then the rule should be stated in a positive way: "Keep hands to self." Group rules should always define specific behaviors in terms young children will understand (e.g., "Be sure to use Nice Talk") and should avoid global constructs (e.g., "Respect others"). Furthermore, it is important to post these rules in picture format to remind the children of the teacher's expectations and to spend time actually teaching these rules to be sure that they are understood. The rules should then be reviewed at the beginning of each group session and periodically during the session until they are well remembered by the children. To facilitate this learning, the number of rules should be few—three or four is a good number with which to begin. (For sample group guidelines, see Figure 20.)

Establishing clearly defined rules in the early stages of group work may prevent many behavior problems. Providing positive reinforcement for obeying the rules (e.g., "Terrific—you used Nice Talk!") will increase the likelihood that rules will be followed.

FIGURE 20 Sample Group Guidelines

1. Toys in cubby

2. Use Nice Talk

3. Keep hands to yourself

4. Listen

Step 2: Anticipate, Prompt, Simplify

The teacher should take steps to anticipate problems in the classroom and then prompt the desirable behavior. Prompting, or telling the children what to do in a given situation, can minimize behavior problems and also provides a positive, encouraging learning environment. For example, if a group of five children are each given paper and scissors but are given only two bottles of glue, it is important that the teacher anticipate the problem of sharing the glue and remind the group to share. Additional practice in asking for the glue (i.e., what words to use) will also likely be needed. Once specific prosocial skills are learned, the children may be prompted to use them. In the situation just described, for example, the teacher might prompt skill use by saying, "Remember to use Asking a Favor (Skill 7) when you need the glue. Who remembers the steps to this skill?"

During Skillstreaming instruction, one of the teacher's main functions is to anticipate difficulties and be ready to prompt a desirable response during role-play activities. Children practicing a new skill in a session may easily forget a step or several steps, or they may not know how to behave in order to carry out a particular step during a role play. The teacher may then give instructional comments or hints to elicit the behavior or coach the children in the skill from start to finish.

Children's abilities to handle particular group participation tasks will vary. Some may have difficulty following a series of instructions or understanding the meaning of instructions. For these children, it would be helpful to present fewer instructions at one time or to repeat instructions, rephrasing them in language that the children can more easily understand. In addition, any task may be divided into a sequence of steps that the children can perform one at a time.

Step 3: Reward Positive Behavior

Foremost among behavioral management techniques for dealing with problematic behavior in the classroom is positive reinforcement. Many disruptions can be reduced or even eliminated by applying positive reinforcement to desirable class behaviors such as listening, participating, and following the group guidelines. For most children, social reinforcers such as verbal praise will be highly rewarding and will likely increase the performance of a desirable behavior. In other cases, a sticker or other material reward, along with social reinforcement, may be needed to increase the frequency of a desirable behavior.[1]

---

[1] For more discussion of the use of reinforcement, see chapter 2. Table 1 in chapter 2 lists a number of possible material and social reinforcers.

Positive reinforcement also has a powerful effect on a child who is behaving inappropriately if other children who are engaging in desirable behavior are rewarded. For example, if those who are listening are reinforced with verbal praise for their listening, a ripple effect is created, and the inattentive child will most likely begin to listen as well (Kounin, 1977). This strategy allows the teacher to control the group in a positive, helping way and decreases the impulse to nag children to pay attention.

Step 4: Offer Positive Consequences

Reminding the children of the positive consequences of a desirable behavior will often provide the encouragement needed for them to stop the undesirable behavior and engage in a more appropriate one. Offering positive consequences means that the child is told that a specific desirable behavior will earn a given reward. Examples include the following: "When you stop crying, you may play"; "When you are quiet, you may go outside"; or "When you listen, you may have a turn." Some behaviors may need a tangible positive consequence, such as "When you put the markers away, you'll get a happy face." Reminding the children to engage in a specific appropriate behavior to earn a privilege or reward lets them know that positive actions lead to good things – and it does so in an encouraging, helpful way.

Step 5: Inform of Negative Consequences

The majority of minor behavioral difficulties (e.g., inattention, noise making, etc.) will likely be remedied by employing Steps 1–4 of this plan. However, if a child's inappropriate behavior does not cease, it may be necessary to inform her of the negative consequence if she chooses to continue the inappropriate behavior. Examples of such negative consequences include sitting away from the group for a minute, not earning a sticker or happy face, or not having a privilege such as playing with a given toy. Such consequences should be as logically related to the misbehavior as possible. For example, if the child misuses a toy, she would then lose the privilege of playing with that toy. Informing the child of the negative consequence thus provides a warning of what will happen if she continues to engage in that behavior.

Step 6: Enforce Negative Consequences

The negative consequence explained to the child is then carried out in a calm and firm manner if the child continues the undesirable behavior. For example, if the child continues to disrupt the Skillstreaming group by making noises and the consequence for this behavior is to sit away from the group for a minute, then the child is required to follow through with this consequence. It is important to stress that once a child has earned a reward for a given positive behavior (e.g., a sticker for listening), that reward should not be taken away as a negative consequence for another undesirable behavior. Loss of a reward previously earned is inappropriate at this age level and may result in more severe maladaptive behavior, such as aggression.

It is important to emphasize that, once the negative consequence has been enforced, the teacher should reevaluate the structure of the learning environment. Possible changes might include seating the child closer to an adult in the Skillstreaming group (Step 1), prompting the child to engage in the desired behavior (Step 2), and providing reinforcement for behaving in a positive manner (Step 3). The example given in the following pages illustrates how these steps may be used.

EXAMPLE

Situation: In the Skillstreaming group, Billy frequently talks out in a loud voice at times when he is not directly engaged in role playing or feedback.

Step 1

The teacher tightens the structure of the group by having Billy sit next to one of the group leaders. When the other children are role playing, she asks Billy to help by pointing to the steps of the skill on the skill chart. Anticipating that Billy may talk out in the group, the teacher reviews the steps to the skill of Listening (Skill 1) and Using Nice Talk (Skill 2) and encourages all group members to follow these group rules.

Step 2

When Billy begins to speak out loudly, the teacher prompts him nonverbally by touching her ear to indicate that he should use the skill of Listening.

Step 3

Billy begins to listen, and the teacher makes a special effort to look at him, smile, and nod her head. When Billy begins to talk loudly again, the teacher rewards those who are listening by saying, "Ann, Jennifer, Lee, good job listening!" As soon as Billy shows that he is listening, the teacher praises him: "Billy, good listening!"

Step 4

Billy begins talking again almost immediately. The teacher then tells him, "When you show you are listening, you may have a turn to role play."

Step 5

Billy continues to talk loudly. The teacher calmly walks over to Billy, saying "Billy, you need to stop talking. You need to listen. If you continue to talk, you won't earn a turn to role play."

Step 6

Billy continues to talk out. The teacher says, "I'm going to choose someone who has been listening for our next role play" and selects another child for the role play, thus enforcing the negative consequence. As soon as Billy begins listening, the teacher selects him as a role-play participant.

Typically, continuing to reward others for listening while ignoring Billy's talking would have provided enough encouragement for him to stop talking and listen. Indeed, for most children, the behavior of talking out would have stopped long before reaching Step 6.

INDIVIDUAL INTERVENTIONS

The majority of commonly occurring problems can be effectively dealt with by employing the strategies in the plan just described. However, for negative behaviors that occur frequently and/or interrupt the learning environment, or for more severe behavior problems, an individual management plan is indicated. For problems such as aggression (hitting, pinching, etc.), an immediate consequence is necessary.

Time-Out

The immediate consequence most commonly used in preschools and kindergartens is time-out. Time-out is an extinction technique that involves removing the child from positive reinforcement (e.g., attention) when other forms of extinction (e.g., ignoring) have been unsuccessful. Most often, time-out involves removing the disruptive child from the on-going activity to sit on a chair in a specified area of the classroom. This procedure should only be used after children have been forewarned of the specific behaviors that will warrant its use and when other management techniques have failed. It should be used only as a last resort because it removes the child not only from positive reinforcement, but also from the learning environment.

For the preschool or kindergarten child, the time-out condition should not exceed 2 minutes. This is long enough to convey to the child the inappropriateness of the behavior for which time-out is the consequence. Using time-out for any longer than the recommended 2 minutes will likely result in the child's exhibiting undesirable behavior while in time-out, which then requires teacher intervention. This teacher attention, even though negative, may be perceived by the child to be rewarding. In addition, when the child returns to the instructional setting, it is critical that she receive positive reinforcement immediately for any type of appropriate behavior. The teacher must create an environment where the child wants to be, or the child may actually begin to see time-out as a positive alternative.

Other Individual Plans

At times, more systematic, structured behavior management plans are needed to create a desired change in individual children's problematic behaviors. When indicated by the intensity or frequency of the behavior, such a plan can be designed by following these steps: First, identify the target behavior to be changed. To do this, list the child's problematic behaviors. Then choose one behavior to decrease in frequency. This may be the behavior that bothers you the most as a teacher, the one that would be the easiest to change, or the one creating the greatest problem for the child.

Second, determine the positive behavior that is incompatible with the undesirable one. For example, if the undesirable behavior is not following directions, the incompatible behavior would be following directions. Obtain baseline data to determine (1) how frequently the undesirable behavior occurs, (2) how frequently the incompatible behavior occurs, and (3) under what conditions each behavior occurs. This process need not be complicated. For example, you may list the undesirable behavior and the incompatible behavior and make a tally mark for each occurrence of the behavior on a given day. Or you may find an A-B-C format useful (specifying the *antecedent* conditions under which the behavior occurred, the specific *behavior* exhibited by the child, and the *consequences* that the child receives as a result of that behavior). The A-B-C's can be written on a sheet of paper and quickly documented whenever the behavior of concern and the incompatible behavior are observed.

Third, determine an effective reinforcer and deliver it consistently. Determining the reinforcer can most effectively be done by watching for the activities that the child seems to particularly enjoy. Deciding on the frequency of reinforcement delivery is next: If the reward is given immediately following the performance of the desirable behavior, it is more likely that the behavior will be repeated. Consequently, some type of small reinforcement (e.g., verbal encouragement along with a sticker or happy face) should be given immediately following the behavior the teacher wants to increase. For many young children, this immediate reinforcement may be all that is needed to create the desired behavior change. However, to teach young children to accept a delay in reinforcement, it is often useful to provide an additional, larger reward (e.g., a special privilege) to be given after the child earns a certain number of stickers or happy faces. A chart to track the child's progress – perhaps a space-ship divided into segments or a ladder with spaces for each sticker – can provide additional encouragement.

Finally, once the individual plan has been implemented, monitor behavior change. Teacher observations and recording of the frequency of both the problematic and incompatible behaviors will provide information on the degree to which desired behavioral changes are in fact occurring.

RELATIONSHIP-BASED TECHNIQUES

Psychologists and educators have long known that the better the relationship between the helper and client or child, the more positive and productive the outcome of their interaction. In fact, some would hold that the establishment and maintenance of a positive relationship is the most potent factor in effecting behavior change in the child. The techniques next described draw primarily upon the relationship between teacher and child. These can often be combined with other classroom management techniques for maximum effect.

Empathic Encouragement

Using this technique, the teacher first shows that he understands the difficulty the child is experiencing and then urges the child to participate as instructed. Often this additional one-to-one attention will provide the child with heightened motivation to follow the teacher's directions. In applying this technique, the teacher first listens to the child explain the problem and expresses an understanding of the child's feelings and behavior (e.g., "I know it's hard. It can be frustrating to learn something new."). If appropriate, the teacher responds that the child's view is an acceptable alternative to deal with the problem. The teacher then restates his own view with supporting reasons and probable outcomes and urges the child to try out the suggestion (e.g., "But if you don't try the skill, you won't know if you could do it. Let's give it a try.").

Threat Reduction

Children may find role playing or other types of participation in Skill-streaming sessions to be anxiety provoking or threatening. If so, they may react with inappropriate or disruptive behaviors or withdraw. To prevent this problem, the teacher should create a supportive environment in which the children need not be embarrassed to try practicing new skills. The teacher should provide reassurance or even physical contact (e.g., an arm around the child, a hug, etc.). The teacher should also encourage the group to express support for role-play volunteers and others who participate.

An Encouraging Environment

The atmosphere of the Skillstreaming group, and the classroom as well, should be encouraging. By this we mean that the teacher should notice the children following the group rules, making prosocial choices, and "being good," rather than catching them breaking rules. Although it is impossible to expect any person to be positive all of the time, a helpful rule to follow is to offer four positive or encouraging statements for each negative statement or reprimand. A benefit of this approach is the fact that when a teacher sees a child behaving appropriately and states approval of that behavior publicly, children who are engaging in unacceptable behavior are likely to stop the unacceptable behavior and engage in the one that received teacher approval (Kounin, 1977).

Behavioral Redirection

One useful way of encouraging a child's appropriate behavior while preventing the occurrence of negative behavior is to employ behavioral redirection, or engage the child in an appropriate or constructive form of the misbehavior or in a different type of activity. For example, a child who frequently disrupts the Skillstreaming group by standing up and walking around may be requested to assist the teacher in pointing out the skill steps as they are being role played. Another example of behavioral redirection would be requesting that a child who inappropriately brings a toy to the group take other classroom materials and put them on the teacher's desk, replacing the toy on the way. This technique thus allows the teacher to emphasize the child's positive, helping actions without ignoring the child's negative or nonconstructive behaviors.

SUMMARY

Problematic behaviors in Skillstreaming groups are those behaviors that interfere with or detract from the group's process as an active, facilitative learning environment. We have described a variety of techniques for dealing with specific types of problematic behaviors. All of these techniques share the common goal of helping the skill-deficient child become actively involved in Skillstreaming so that the skills being taught can be learned and practiced effectively.

References

Alevizos, K., Labrecque, V. H., & Gregersen, G. F. (1972). *Effects of area size on play behaviors.* Salt Lake City: Children's Behavior Therapy Unit, Salt Lake City Mental Health.

Allen, K. E., Benning, P. M., & Drummond, T. W. (1972). Integration of normal and handicapped children in a behavior modification preschool: A case study. In G. Jemb (Ed.), *Behavior analysis and education.* Lawrence: University of Kansas Press.

Alvord, M. K. (1978). The effects of non-motion symbolic modeling on the sharing behavior of young children. (Doctoral Dissertation, University of Maryland, 1977). *Dissertation Abstracts International, 39,* 764–765A.

Asher, S. R., & Hymel, S. (1981). Children's social competence in peer relations: Sociometric and behavioral assessment. In J. Wine & M. Smye (Eds.), *Social competence.* New York: Guilford.

Asher, S. R., Singleton, L. C., Tinsley, B. R., & Hymel, S. (1979). A reliable sociometric measure for preschool children. *Developmental Psychology, 15,* 443–444.

Asher, S. R., & Taylor, A. R. (1982). Social outcomes of mainstreaming: Sociometric assessment and beyond. In P. S. Strain (Ed.), *Social development of exceptional children.* Rockville, MD: Aspen Systems.

Bandura, A. (1977). *Social learning theory.* Englewood Cliffs, NJ: Prentice-Hall.

Bandura, A., Ross, D., & Ross, S. A. (1961). Transmission of aggression through imitation of aggressive models. *Journal of Abnormal and Social Psychology, 63,* 575–582.

Barclay, J. (1966). Interest patterns associated with measures of desirability. *Personality Guidance Journal, 45,* 56–60.

Barton, E. J. (1981). Developing sharing: An analysis of modeling and other behavioral techniques. *Behavior Modification, 5,* 386–398.

Behar, L. B. (1977). The Preschool Behavior Questionnaire. *Journal of Abnormal Child Psychology, 5,* 265–275.

Brown, L. L., & Hammill, D. D. (1978). *Behavior Rating Profile: An ecological approach to behavioral assessment.* Austin, TX: PRO-ED.

Brown, P., & Elliott, R. (1965). Control of aggression in a nursery school class. *Journal of Experimental Child Psychology, 2,* 103–107.

Bryan, T. S., & Bryan, J. H. (1978). Social interactions of learning disabled children. *Learning Disabilities Quarterly, 1,* 33–38.

Buckley, N. K., & Walker, H. M. (1978). *Modifying classroom behavior: A manual of procedure for classroom teachers* (rev. ed.). Champaign, IL: Research Press.

Buhremester, D. (1982). *Children's Concerns Inventory manual.* Los Angeles: University of California, Department of Psychiatry.

Burstein, N. D. (1986). The effects of classroom organization on mainstream preschool children. *Exceptional Children, 52,* 425–434.

Callantine, M. F., & Warren, L. M. (1955). Learning sets in human concept formation. *Psychological Reports, 1,* 363–367.

Camp, B. W., & Bash, M. A. S. (1981). *Think aloud: Increasing social and cognitive skills—A problem-solving program for children* (Primary Level). Champaign, IL: Research Press.

Camp, B. W., & Bash, M. A. S. (1985). *Think aloud: Increasing social and cognitive skills—A problem-solving program for children* (Classroom Program, Grades 1–2). Champaign, IL: Research Press.

Campbell, S. B. (1974). Cognitive styles and behavior problems of clinic boys: A comparison of epileptic, hyperactive, learning disabled, and normal groups. *Journal of Abnormal Child Psychology, 2,* 307–312.

Cartledge, G., & Milburn, J. F. (1980). *Teaching social skills to children.* New York: Pergamon.

Chan, K. S., & Rueda, R. (1979). Poverty and culture in education: Separate but equal. *Exceptional Children, 45,* 422–428.

Chesler, M., & Fox, R. (1966). *Role playing methods in the classroom.* Chicago: Science Research Associates.

Coie, J. D. (1985). Fitting social skills intervention to the target group. In B. H. Schneider, K. H. Rubin, & J. E. Ledingham (Eds.), *Children's peer relations: Issues in assessment and intervention.* New York: Springer-Verlag.

Coie, J. D., Dodge, K. A., & Coppotelli, H. (1982). Dimensions and types of social status: A cross-age perspective. *Developmental Psychology, 18,* 557–570.

Coie, J. D., & Kupersmidt, J. B. (1983). A behavioral analysis of emerging social status in boys' groups. *Child Development, 54,* 1400–1416.

Connolly, J., & Doyle, A. (1981). Assessment of social competence in preschoolers: Teachers versus peers. *Developmental Psychology, 17,* 454–462.

Connors, K. (1975). *Revised Connor's Rating Scale.* Chicago: Abbott Laboratories.

Cooke, T., & Apolloni, T. (1976). Developing positive social-emotional behaviors: A study of training and generalization effects. *Journal of Applied Behavior Analysis, 9,* 65–78.

Cowen, E. L., Pederson, A., Babigian, H., Izzo, L. D., & Trost, M. A. (1973). Long-term follow-up of early detected vulnerable children. *Journal of Consulting and Clinical Psychology, 41,* 438–446.

Davis, K., & Jones, E. E. (1960). Changes in interpersonal perception as a means of reducing cognitive dissonance. *Journal of Abnormal and Social Psychology, 61,* 402–410.

Dodge, K. A. (1983). Behavioral antecedents of peer social status. *Child Development, 54,* 1385–1399.

Dodge, K. A. (1985). Facets of social interaction and the assessment of social competence in children. In B. H. Schneider, K. H. Rubin, & J. E. Ledingham (Eds.), *Children's peer relations: Issues in assessment and intervention.* New York: Springer-Verlag.

Dodge, K. A., Coie, J. D., & Bralke, N. P. (1982). Behavior patterns of socially rejected and neglected preadolescents: The roles of social approach and aggression. *Journal of Abnormal Child Psychology, 10,* 389–410.

Dodge, K. A., Schlundt, D. G., Schoken, I., & Dehugach, J. D. (1983). Social competence and children's sociometric status: The role of peer group entry strategies. *Merrill-Palmer Quarterly, 29,* 309–336.

Dowrick, P. W. (1986). *Social survival for children: A trainer's resource book.* New York: Brunner/Mazel.

Duncan, C. P. (1958). Transfer after training with single versus multiple tasks. *Journal of Experimental Psychology, 55,* 63–73.

Evers, W. L., & Schwarz, J. C. (1973). Modifying social withdrawal in preschoolers: The effects of filmed modeling and teacher praise. *Journal of Abnormal Psychology, 1,* 248–256.

Evers-Pasquale, W. L. (1978). The peer preference test as a measure of reward value: Item analysis, cross-validation, concurrent validation, and replication. *Journal of Abnormal Child Psychology, 6,* 175–188.

Evers-Pasquale, W. L., & Sherman, M. (1975). A variable influencing the efficacy of filmed modeling in modifying social isolation in preschoolers. *Journal of Abnormal Child Psychology, 3,* 179–189.

Fairchild, L., & Erwin, W. M. (1977). Physical punishment by parent figures as a model of aggressive behavior in children. *Journal of Genetic Psychology, 130,* 279–284.

Federal Register. (1975). Public Law 94–142, Education for All Handicapped Children Act of 1975.

Forehand, R., & King, H. E. (1977). Noncompliant children: Effects of parent training on behavior and attitude change. *Behavior Modification, 1,* 93–108.

Foster, S. L., & Ritchey, W. L. (1979). Issues in the assessment of social competence in children. *Journal of Applied Behavior Analysis, 12,* 625–638.

Foster, S. L., & Ritchey, W. L. (1983). *Behavioral correlates of sociometric status of fourth, fifth, and sixth grade children in two classroom situations.* Unpublished manuscript.

Goldstein, A. P. (1973). *Structured learning therapy: Toward a psychotherapy for the poor.* New York: Academic.

Goldstein, A. P. (1981). *Psychological skill training.* Elmsford, NY: Pergamon.

Goldstein, A. P., Sprafkin, R. P., & Gershaw, N. J. (1976). *Skill training for community living: Applying structured learning therapy.* Elmsford, NY: Pergamon.

Goldstein, A. P., Sprafkin, R. P., Gershaw, N. J., & Klein, P. (1980). *Skillstreaming the adolescent: A structured learning approach to teaching prosocial skills.* Champaign, IL: Research Press.

Gottman, J. M. (1977). Toward a definition of social isolation in children. *Child Development, 48,* 513–517.

Gottman, J. M. (1983). How children become friends. *Monographs of the Society for Research in Child Development, 48* (3, Serial No. 201).

Gouze, K., Gordon, L., & Rayias, M. (1983, April). *Information processing correlates of aggression: A look at attention and memory.* Paper presented at the biennial meeting of the Society for Research in Child Development, Detroit.

Green, K. D., Forehand, R., Beck, S. J., & Vosk, B. (1980). An assessment of the relationship among measures of children's social competence and children's academic achievement. *Child Development, 51,* 1149–1156.

Greenwood, C. R., Todd, N. M., Hops, H., & Walker, H. M. (1982). Behavior change targets in the assessment and treatment of socially withdrawn preschool children. *Behavioral Assessment, 4,* 273–297.

Greenwood, C. R., Walker, H. M., & Hops, H. (1977). Issues in social interaction/withdrawal assessment. *Exceptional Children, 43,* 490–499.

Greenwood, C. R., Walker, H. M., Todd, N. M., & Hops, H. (1978). *Description of withdrawn children's behavior in preschool settings* (Report No. 40). Eugene: University of Oregon, Center at Oregon for Research in the Behavioral Education of the Handicapped.

Greenwood, C. R., Walker, H. M., Todd, N., & Hops, H. (1979). Selecting a cost-effective screening measure for the assessment of preschool social withdrawal. *Journal of Applied Behavior Analysis, 12,* 639–652.

Gresham, F. M. (1981). Assessment of children's social skills. *Journal of School Psychology, 19,* 120–133.

Gresham, F. M. (1982). Misguided mainstreaming: The case for social skills training with handicapped children. *Exceptional Children, 48,* 422–433.

Gresham, F. M. (1983). Multitrait-multimethod approach to multifactored assessment: Theoretical rationale and practical applications. *School Psychology Review, 12*, 26–34.

Gresham, F. M. (1984). Social skills and self-efficacy for exceptional children. *Exceptional Children, 51*, 253–261.

Gronlund, N. E. (1951). *The accuracy of teacher's judgements concerning the sociometric status of sixth grade pupils* (Sociometry Monographs No. 25). New York: Beacon.

Gronlund, N. E., & Anderson, L. (1957). Personality characteristics of socially accepted, socially neglected, and socially rejected junior high school pupils. *Educational Administration and Supervision, 43*, 329–338.

Grusec, J. E., Kuczynski, L., Rushton, J. P., & Simutis, Z. M. (1978). Modeling, direct instruction and attributions: Effects on altruism. *Developmental Psychology, 14*, 51–57.

Hartup, W. W. (1970). Peer interaction and social organization. In P. H. Mussen (Ed.), *Carmichael's manual of child psychology* (Vol. 2). New York: Wiley.

Hartup, W. W. (1983). Peer relations. In P. H. Mussen (Ed.), *Handbook of child psychology* (Vol. 4). New York: Wiley.

Hartup, W. W., Glazer, J., & Charlesworth, R. (1967). Peer reinforcement and sociometric status. *Child Development, 38*, 1017–1024.

Hops, H. (1982). Behavioral assessment of exceptional children's social development. In P. S. Strain (Ed.), *Social development of exceptional children*. Rockville, MD: Aspen Systems.

Hops, H., Fleischman, D. H., Guild, J., Paine, S., Street, A., Walker, H. M., & Greenwood, C. R. (1978). *Program for establishing effective relationship skills (PEERS): Consultant manual*. Eugene: University of Oregon, Center at Oregon for Research in the Behavioral Education of the Handicapped.

Hubbel, A. (1954). Two person role-playing for guidance in social readjustment. *Group Psychotherapy, 7*, 249–254.

Hymel, S., & Asher, S. H. (1977). *Assessment and training of isolated children's social skills*. Bethesda, MD: National Institute of Child Health and Human Development.

Iwata, B. A., & Bailey, J. S. (1974). Reward versus cost token systems: An analysis of the effects on students and teacher. *Journal of Applied Behavior Analysis, 7*, 567–576.

Janes, C. L., & Hesselbrock, V. (1978). Problem children's adult adjustment predicted from teacher's ratings. *American Journal of Orthopsychiatry, 48*, 300–309.

Janes, C. L., Hesselbrock, V., Myers, D., & Penniman, J. (1979). Problem boys in young adulthood: Teachers' ratings and twelve-year follow up. *Journal of Youth and Adolescence, 8*, 453–472.

Jennings, K. D. (1975). People versus object orientation, social behavior, and intellectual abilities in children. *Developmental Psychology, 11,* 511–519.

Johnson, D. W., & Johnson, R. T. (1986). *Learning together and alone* (2nd ed.). Englewood Cliffs, NJ: Prentice-Hall.

Kane, J. S., & Lawler, E. E. (1978). Methods of peer assessment. *Psychological Bulletin, 85,* 555–586.

Kaufman, J. M., Gordon, M. E., & Baker, A. (1978). Being imitated: Persistence of an effect. *Journal of Genetic Psychology, 132,* 319–320.

Keller, F. M., & Carlson, P. M. (1974). The use of symbolic modeling to promote social skills in children with low levels of social responsiveness. *Child Development, 45,* 912–919.

Keogh, B. K., & Burnstein, J. D. (1988). Relationship of temperament to preschoolers' interaction with peers and teachers. *Exceptional Children, 54,* 456–461.

Kirby, F. D., & Toler, H. C. (1970). Modifications of preschool isolate behavior: A case study. *Journal of Applied Behavior Analysis, 3,* 303–314.

Kirkland, K. D., & Thelen, M. H. (1977). Uses of modeling in child treatment. In B. B. Lahey & A. E. Kazden (Eds.), *Advances in clinical psychology.* New York: Plenum.

Kohlberg, L., LaCrosse, J., & Ricks, D. (1972). The predictability of adult mental health from childhood behavior. In B. Wolman (Ed.), *Manual of child psychopathology.* New York: McGraw-Hill.

Kohn, M. (1977). *Social competence, symptoms and underachievement in childhood: A longitudinal perspective.* Washington, DC: Winston.

Kohn, M., & Rosman, B. L. (1972). Relationship of preschool social-emotional functioning to later intellectual achievement. *Developmental Psychology, 6,* 445–452.

Kounin, J. (1977). *Discipline and group management in classrooms.* Huntington, NY: Krieger.

Krantz, M. (1982). Sociometric awareness, social participation, and perceived popularity in preschool children. *Child Development, 53,* 376–379.

Kupersmidt, J. B. (1983, April). Predicting delinquency and academic problems from childhood peer status. In J. D. Coie (Chair), *Strategies for identifying children at social risk: Longitudinal correlates and consequences.* Symposium conducted at the biennial meeting of the Society for Research in Child Development, Detroit.

Lesser, G. (1959). The relationship between various forms of aggression and popularity among lower-class children. *Journal of Educational Psychology, 50,* 20–25.

Lichtenstein, E., Keutzer, C. S., & Himes, K. H. (1969). Emotional role-playing and changes in smoking attitudes and behaviors. *Psychological Reports, 23,* 379–387.

Lowe, M. L., & Cuvo, A. J. (1976). Teaching coin summation to the mentally retarded. *Journal of Applied Behavior Analysis, 9,* 483–489.

Maccoby, E. E. (1980). *Social development.* New York: Harcourt Brace Jovanovitch.

Mann, J. H. (1956). Experimental evaluations of role-playing. *Psychological Bulletin, 53,* 227–234.

Marshall, H., & McCandless, B. (1957). A study in prediction of social behavior of preschool children. *Child Development, 28,* 149–159.

Matson, J. L., Rotatori, A. F., & Helsel, W. J. (1983). Development of a rating scale to measure social skills in children: The Matson Evaluation of Social Skills with Youngsters (MESSY). *Behaviour Research and Therapy, 21,* 335–340.

Mayer, M. (1983). *I was so mad.* Racine, WI: Western.

McCandless, B., & Marshall, H. (1957). A picture sociometric technique for preschool children. *Child Development, 28,* 149–159.

McCarthy, J. M., & Paraskevopoulos, J. (1969). Behavior patterns of learning disabled, emotionally disturbed, and average children. *Exceptional Children, 36,* 69–74.

McConnell, S. R., Strain, P. S., Kerr, M. M., Staff, V., Lenkner, D. A., & Lambert, D. L. (1984). An empirical definition of social adjustment: Selection of target behaviors for a comprehensive treatment program. *Behavior Modification, 8,* 451–473.

McGehee, N., & Thayer, P. W. (1961). *Training in business and industry.* New York: Wiley.

McGinnis, E., Goldstein, A. P., Sprafkin, R. P., & Gershaw, N. J. (1984). *Skillstreaming the elementary school child: A guide for teaching prosocial skills.* Champaign, IL: Research Press.

Milich, R., & Landau, S. (1982). Socialization and peer relations in hyperactive children. In K. D. Gadow & I. Bialer (Eds.), *Advances in learning and behavioral disorders.* Greenwich, CT: JAI.

Mize, J., & Ladd, G. W. (1984, April). Preschool children's goal and strategy knowledge: A comparison of picture-story and enactive assessment. In G. W. Ladd (Chair), *From preschool to high school: Are children's interpersonal goals and strategies predictive of their social competence?* Symposium conducted at the annual meeting of the American Educational Research Association, New Orleans.

Moreno, J. L. (1934). *Who shall survive?* Washington, DC: Nervous and Mental Disease Publishing.

Murphy, J. B. (1985). *Feelings.* Ontario: Black Moss.

Nichols, H. (1954). Role-playing in primary grades. *Group Psychotherapy, 7,* 238–241.

Norquist, V. M., & Bradley, B. (1973). Speech acquisition in a nonverbal isolate child. *Journal of Experimental Psychology, 15,* 149–160.

O'Connor, R. D. (1969). Modification of social withdrawal through symbolic modeling. *Journal of Applied Behavior Analysis, 2,* 15–22.

Oden, S. (1980). A child's social isolation: Origins, prevention, intervention. In G. Cartledge & J. F. Milburn (Eds.), *Teaching social skills to children.* New York: Pergamon.

Oden, S., & Asher, S. R. (1977). Coaching children in social skills for friendship making. *Child Development, 48,* 495–506.

O'Leary, K. D., & Johnson, S. B. (1979). Psychological assessment. In N. C. Quay & J. Werry (Eds.), *Psychopathological disorders of childhood.* New York: Wiley.

Parker, J., & Asher, S. R. (1985). *Peer acceptance and later personal adjustment: Are low-accepted children "at risk"?* Unpublished manuscript, University of Illinois at Urbana-Champaign.

Patterson, G. R. (1982). *Coercive family process.* Eugene, OR: Castalia.

Peery, M. A. (1979). *Didactic instructions for and modeling of empathy.* Unpublished doctoral dissertation, Syracuse University, NY.

Piaget, J. (1962). *Play, dreams, and imitation in childhood.* New York: Norton.

Piper, W. (1976). *The little engine that could.* New York: Platt & Munk.

Putallaz, M., & Gottman, J. M. (1981). An interactional model of children's entry into peer groups. *Child Development, 52,* 986–994.

Quay, H. C. (1979). Classification. In H. C. Quay & J. Werry (Eds.), *Psychopathological disorders of childhood.* New York: Wiley.

Quilitch, H. R., & Risley, T. R. (1973). The effects of play materials on social play. *Journal of Applied Behavior Analysis, 6,* 573–578.

Rathjen, D., Hiniker, A., & Rathjen, E. (1976). *Incorporation of behavioral techniques in a game format to teach children social skills.* Paper presented at the meeting of the Association for Advancement of Behavior Therapy, New York.

Roff, M., Sells, S. B., & Golden, M. (1972). *Social adjustment and personality development in children.* Minneapolis: University of Minnesota Press.

Rogers-Warren, A., & Baer, D. M. (1976). Correspondence between saying and doing: Teaching children to share and praise. *Journal of Applied Behavior Analysis, 9,* 335–354.

Rolf, J. (1976). Peer status and the directionality of symptomatic behavior: Prime social competence predictors of outcome for vulnerable children. *American Journal of Orthopsychiatry, 46,* 74–88.

Rosenthal, T. L. (1976). Modeling therapies. In M. Hersen, R. M. Eisler, & P. M. Miller (Eds.), *Progress in behavior modification* (Vol. 2). New York: Academic.

Ross, D. M., Ross, S. A., & Evans, T. A. (1976). The modification of extreme social withdrawal by modeling with guided participation. *Journal of Behavior Therapy and Experimental Psychiatry, 2,* 273–279.

Schneider, B. H., & Byrne, B. M. (1985). Children's social skills training: A meta-analysis. In B. H. Schneider, K. H. Rubin, & J. E. Ledingham (Eds.), *Children's peer relations: Issues in assessment and intervention.* New York: Springer-Verlag.

Schneider, M., & Robin, A. (1974). *Turtle Manual.* Stony Brook: State University of New York, Psychology Department.

Shoabs, N. E. (1964). Role playing in the individual psychotherapy interview. *Journal of Individual Psychology, 26,* 84–89.

Shore, E., & Sechrest, L. (1961). Concept attainment as a function of number of positive instances presented. *Journal of Educational Psychology, 52,* 303–307.

Shure, M. B., & Spivack, G. (1980). Interpersonal problem solving as a mediator of behavioral adjustment in preschool and kindergarten children. *Journal of Applied Developmental Psychology, 1,* 29–44.

Singleton, L. C., & Asher, S. R. (1977). Peer preferences and social interaction among third grade children in an integrated school district. *Journal of Educational Psychology, 69,* 330–336.

Slaby, R. G., & Crowley, C. G. (1977). Modification of cooperation and aggression through teacher attention to children's speech. *Journal of Experimental Child Psychology, 23,* 442–458.

Spivack, G. E., Platt, J. J., & Shure, M. B. (1976). *The problem-solving approach to adjustment.* San Francisco: Jossey-Bass.

Spivack, G. E., & Shure, M. B. (1974). *Social adjustment of young children.* San Francisco: Jossey-Bass.

Staub, E. (1971). The use of role playing and induction in children's learning of helping and sharing behavior. *Child Development, 42,* 805–816.

Stephens, T. M. (1978). *Social skills in the classroom.* Columbus, OH: Cedars.

Stephens, T. M. (1980). *Social Behavior Assessment.* Columbus, OH: Cedars.

Stokes, T. F., & Baer, D. M. (1977). An implicit technology of generalization. *Journal of Applied Behavior Analysis, 10,* 349–368.

Stokes, T. F., Baer, D. M., & Jackson, R. L. (1974). Programming the generalization of a greeting response in four retarded children. *Journal of Applied Behavior Analysis, 7,* 599–610.

Strain, P. S. (1977). Increasing social play of severely retarded preschoolers with sociodramatic activities. *Mental Retardation, 13,* 7–9.

Strain, P. S. (1981). *The utilization of classroom peers as behavior change agents.* New York: Plenum.

Strain, P. S., & Odom, S. L. (1986). Peer social initiations: Effective intervention for social development of exceptional children. *Exceptional Children, 52,* 543–552.

Strain, P. S., Shores, R. E., & Timm, M. A. (1977). Effects of peer social initiations on the behavior of withdrawn pre-school children. *Journal of Applied Behavior Analysis, 10,* 289–298.

Swift, M., & Spivack, G. E. (1969). Clarifying the relationship between academic success and overt classroom behavior. *Exceptional Children, 36,* 99–104.

Toner, I. J., Moore, L. P., & Ashley, P. K. (1978). The effect of serving as a model of self-control on subsequent resistance to deviation in children. *Journal of Experimental Psychology, 26,* 85–91.

U. S. House of Representatives. (1986). *Education of the Handicapped Act Amendments of 1986* (Report No. 99–860). Washington, DC: U. S. Government Printing Office.

Van Hasselt, V. B., Bellack, A. S., & Hersen, M. (1979). *The relationship between behavioral assessment and sociometric status of children.* Paper presented at the annual meeting of the Association for Advancement of Behavior Therapy, San Francisco.

Van Hasselt, V. B., Hersen, M., & Bellack, A. S. (1981). The validity of role play tests for assessing social skills in children. *Behavior Therapy, 12,* 202–216.

Wahler, R. G. (1967). Setting generality: Some specific and general effects of child behavior therapy. *Journal of Applied Behavior Analysis, 2,* 239–246.

Walker, H. M. (1979). *The acting out child: Coping with classroom disruptions.* Boston: Allyn & Bacon.

Walker, H. M., McConnel, S., Holmes, D., Todis, B., Walker, J., & Golden, N. (1983). *The Walker Social Skills Curriculum: The ACCEPTS Program.* Austin, TX: PRO-ED.

Walker, R. (1967). Some temperament traits in children as viewed by their peers, their teachers, and themselves. *Monographs of the Society for Research in Child Development, 32,* 1–36.

Wanlas, R. L., & Prinz, R. J. (1982). Methodological issues in conceptualizing and treating childhood social isolation. *Psychological Review, 92,* 39–55.

Weir, K., Stevenson, J., & Graham, P. (1980). Behavior deviance and teacher ratings of prosocial behavior. *American Academy of Child Psychiatry, 19,* 68–77.

Zimmerman, B. J., & Dialissi, F. (1973). Modeling influences on children's creative behavior. *Journal of Educational Psychology, 65,* 127–134.

Author Index

Subject Index

About the Authors

After earning her PhD in Behavior Disorders in 1986, *Ellen McGinnis* served as Assistant Professor of Special Education at the University of Wisconsin–Eau Claire. In addition to being a special education consultant in both public school and hospital based programs, she has taught in the public schools for 11 years. She is currently a teacher of behaviorally disordered adolescents and a training consultant in Des Moines, Iowa. Dr. McGinnis has authored numerous articles related to identifying and teaching behaviorally disordered youth. In addition, she is coauthor with Dr. Arnold P. Goldstein of the book *Skillstreaming the Elementary School Child: A Guide for Teaching Prosocial Skills*. She has two children – Sara, age 7, and Alex, age 3.

Arnold P. Goldstein, PhD, joined the clinical psychology section of Syracuse University's Psychology Department in 1963 and both taught there and directed its Psychotherapy Center until 1980. In 1981, he founded the Center for Research on Aggression, which he currently directs. He joined Syracuse University's Division of Special Education in 1985. Dr. Goldstein has a career-long interest, as both researcher and practitioner, in difficult-to-reach clients. Since 1980, his main research and psychoeducational focus has been incarcerated juvenile offenders and child-abusing parents. He is the developer of Structured Learning, a psychoeducational program and curriculum designed to teach prosocial behaviors to chronically antisocial persons. Dr. Goldstein's many books include *Structured Learning Therapy: Toward a Psychotherapy for the Poor; Skillstreaming the Adolescent: A Structured Learning Approach to Teaching Prosocial Skills; School Violence; Aggression Replacement Training: A Comprehensive Intervention for Aggressive Youth; The Prepare Curriculum: Teaching Prosocial Competencies;* and *Delinquents on Delinquency.*